So, you THINK you want to FOSTER?

JIM BRYANS

So, you think you want to Foster?

Copyright © 2022 by Jim Bryans.

PB: ISBN: 978-1-63812-446-7
Ebook ISBN: 978-1-63812-447-4

All rights reserved. No part in this book may be produced and transmitted in any form or by any means, electronic, or mechanical, including photocopying, recording, or by any information storage and retrieval system, without permission in writing from the copyright owner.

The views expressed in this work are solely those of the author and do not necessarily reflect the views of the publisher hereby disclaims any responsibility for them.
Published by Pen Culture Solutions 10/04/2022

Pen Culture Solutions
1-888-727-7204 (USA)
1-800-950-458 (Australia)
support@penculturesolutions.com

I ventured into fostering more or less on the directions of my wife, June. She went into it with gusto and initially I tagged along. Our experiences go back over forty-five years.

I was brought up in the care of a really tough children's home, and that gave me insight to both sides of the fence; I was able to equate to both carers, and cared for. June launched into the training side of things, and even sat on adoption panels; she was streets ahead of me. I did partake in some of the training, and I was even on the board of a Children's charity. However, when it came to what made the kids tick, I was in a league of my own. In a lot of cases I knew exactly what they were thinking; so, in a way, June and I complimented each other, and that's the very reason I wrote my book.

I do hope it helps to shed light on some of the difficulties you might experience if you venture into this fascinating profession, or if you've already been there, perhaps it willhelp to know that you are not alone; we havebeen there too.

Jim Bryans.

So, you think you want to Foster?
By
Jim Bryans

Preface.

Having done over forty-five years in fostering, I think I can safely say that I do not know anyone else who has been through the same. No one that I know of has fostered for forty-five years, had a serious allegation, came through it and carried on fostering!

Following the trauma of the allegation, we took part in several TV programs and the making of teaching videos for carers and Social Workers, and ended up lecturing for different authorities. June gave telephone support, nationwide, to families who'd had allegations. The thing that struck me about the lectures; generally speaking, they were attended by ladies, the only men in attendance were social workers, and of course, myself.

Who invariably gets the allegations? The men, or the males in the household! On one of our lectures, we met an American lady who was astonished that I'd had an allegation.

'What happens in America when someone has an allegation?' I asked.

'Over there,' she said, 'When someone has an allegation, they get out of fostering, simple as that!'

It is very much the same here, we seem to be the exception to the rule, which I think bears witness that the allegation was false. The misery that it brought upon us was as bad as a death. The only way I can describe its impact is: a friend of ours had an allegation and was so distraught that he hung himself. We persevered and came through it stronger than ever; I think that makes us pretty unique; no thanks to inept Social Workers!

Fostering?

June and I lost count of the children we fostered many years ago. It all started when we came as refugees with our three children from trouble-torn Northern Ireland. We managed to rent a house in a quite select area in Buckinghamshire. It was a weekend and we were relaxing over coffee.

'Do you know what I'd like to do?' She asked.

I glanced at her and spread my hands.

'I'd like to foster,' she said.

She had mentioned 'fostering' in the past but this was the first time she had actually said she wanted to do it.

'Are you sure? We've already got three kids.'

'I know, but it's something I feel that I would really like to do.'

'So, what are you going to do about it then?'

'I'm going to apply to the Local Council, and we'll see what they have to say…'

She was sitting, elbows on the table, hands clasping her coffee cup, staring out of the patio doors. I met her when she was fifteen years old, she was now twenty-five. 'Ten years,' I thought. She was around five foot four inches tall, auburn hair, green eyes and to me, she was beautiful, I loved her to bits, she was my ideal woman!

'There would be no problem with room,' she said, still deep in thought.

This was a large four-bedroom house. It was all we could get at the time and at a rent of ten pounds a week, it was exorbitant! In 1971, no one paid a weekly rent of ten pounds, this was a time when three pounds was the upper limit on rent.

Belfast was no place to raise a family of small children. Bombings and shootings were commonplace, especially in our area just above Ardoyne, a trouble hotspot. We'd had a couple of near misses, and the house next to ours took a bad blast from a bomb placed in a shop opposite; we would have got it as well, but fortunately, the gable end of our house faced the blast so we were spared. John, our neighbour wasn't so lucky, his windows were blown out and he was blown across the room. His house was a mess; he was badly shaken but escaped pretty well unscathed. Shortly after that, three young soldiers lured to a taxi were shot through the head. That very night, I took June and the children to the boat, and they sailed to England; to her mother's place. I stayed behind in an effort to sell our house, but I couldn't sell it, or claim anything for it. Six months later, I gave up and arranged a lorry driving job with a firm near Leighton Buzzard, and when I arrived in England, I started work straight away. Upon arrival, my first task was to find a house. I attempted to buy many houses, but this was a time of runaway prices and gazumping. During that period, in a very short space of time, property prices soared by many thousands. As time went by, because of rocketing prices, the money that could have set us up initially was just not enough. We couldn't afford to buy; we never did sell our house in Belfast

We visited Ronnie and Sally, friends from way back when we were teenagers, and mentioned our housing problem.

Ronnie said: 'Sally looks after a big house near Aylesbury,'

Sally said: 'It belongs to friends of ours who are abroad. They wanted us to rent it, but who in their right mind would pay rent of ten pounds a week?'

'We'll try anything once.' I said and we signed up for a rent of £43.30 a month. That was how we came to be sitting here drinking coffee and discussing fostering.

As instructed, I made myself available for the social worker who came to assess us. To my surprise, he was a young man - very early twenties - with an air of authority and what I interpreted to be almost hostility.

The third degree began: 'And what makes you think you want to foster?'

'Well,' June said: 'Jim was brought up in care and we feel he had needs that were never met. We have a nice home and room, so if we can help some children out, then that's what we would like to do.'

'But you already have three children; does that not make it all a bit ridiculous? What person in their right mind with three children would want to foster? I think you already have as much, if not more than enough for anyone to cope with.'

The entire meeting went along these lines, and not surprisingly we were turned down. Although she hoped we wouldn't be, we received notice shortly afterwards informing us that we were 'unsuitable.' That's not quite how they put it, but that was what in the end it all boiled down to.

'Who gives a monkey's anyway?' I retorted, 'I wonder what he'd have said if he had known we have three kids... another on the way, and a dog!'

She laughed but it took her quite some time to accept the situation. In the meantime, she went into the local Hospital and we had our fourth child, Peter.

Months later, we were approached by a lady social worker who asked if we would be interested in helping a young unmarried mother and her baby. I wasn't sure about this, although I was prepared to go along with June if she wanted to do it. In those days it was really scorned on to be pregnant out of wedlock. These poor kids - and that's just what they were – kids. Some of them were rejected by their families, some just ran away to hide from the scandalmongers, and others never did have their babies, they found the trauma of a back-street abortion, even in primitive conditions, preferable to being tagged, 'unmarried mothers.'

During the period that followed, we 'fostered' a number of these young girls. In the main, they were pathetic little figures who did their utmost to avoid me. Their stay in each case was very brief - just time to sort their lives out and leave. Even though their stay was brief, this insight into their lives at their time of great need, had a profound effect on me. I swore then that if ever a daughter of mine had an illegitimate child, I would not reject her, but help and assist in every way I could. Nowadays of course, it is commonplace for unmarried couples to have children, so the problems they faced no longer exist.

The lady approached us again and asked if we would be prepared to take a teenage boy, the fifteen-year-old son of a friend who was going home, two hundred and fifty miles north. Adam wanted to stay in the area, and he was the first one that I really regarded as anything akin to fostering. The fact that he was no trouble at all, set him apart from most fostering situations.

In the meantime, I scanned the papers every week in search of property for sale, but felt sure we would never be able to buy. It was hardly surprising that rented properties rocketed in price as well. Each week I noticed several in the property to rent column. One in particular went: 'bungalow to rent, fully furnished, twenty-three pounds per week,' and from then on, these ads appeared regularly.

The next time we saw Sally she said, 'Oh, I'm afraid I've got some bad news for you. Someone sent the people who own your house a local paper and having seen the property page, they say they are not charging you enough rent.'

'Oh God!' I moaned, 'I'm going flat out as it is. If they put it up by much, we won't be able to pay it.'

Sally looked at the floor and moved a pebble with her foot. 'I'm sorry, but it's even worse than that, they say they are going to double it!'

'Well, that's it!' June said, 'We will just have to find another place!'

A few weeks went by and as luck would have it, we managed to get another place. The difference was considerable, it being a small three-bedroom house with a back yard, as opposed to a large house and garden, but we soon settled in. Adam found digs locally, we did see him from time to time and he was doing very well.

The Beginning.

The lady who approached us regarding Adam asked if we would take a teenage girl who was homeless. We did, and I found it very hard to like her, because on several occasions, she arrived home the worse for drink, or drugs - or perhaps both. I thought that was very likely the reason for her being homeless in the first place, and I was not happy for the children to see this.

One night, she came home and to me, she looked to be absolutely blotto. Although, at the time I felt cross, I didn't say anything. She went, as I thought, to bed, and little while later, I went to the bathroom. To my horror, she was sprawled out on the toilet, her knickers round her ankles, her skirt hoisted to her waist, her knees pointing to east and west and her head laid back on the cistern; she was either asleep or unconscious. She had dropped her bag on the floor, and a load of little blue pills had spilled. I grabbed a handful and slammed the bathroom door. As I dashed down the stairs, June was coming out of the living room.

'What is going on here?' I stormed. 'That dopey… well she's flat out on the toilet and what are these?' I held the pills out.

June shook her head, 'I don't know.'

'I don't know either, 'I said,' but I'm going to find out! Can you keep an eye on this situation? I don't want the children to see her in that state. I'm going over to the Police station right now!'

I ran the four or five hundred yards to the Police station and rang the bell. A policewoman came to the hatch: 'Can I help you?'

I poured the pills onto the counter, 'What are these?'

She peered at them for a few seconds and shrugged, 'I don't know.'

I said, 'I need to see someone who can tell me what they are, because, I have reason to believe that a young girl at my house is in a serious condition with these - and goodness knows what else.' I dashed back home and the Police arrived almost immediately. They said that she should be medically examined as her condition was very strange. We assume they took her to the Hospital. As required, we notified Social Services; she never did return, and we were never informed about her, or where she went. I found that very odd, but if I am honest, I was quite relieved.

During the period that followed, we had two more children of our own, making six in all, so with the larger family, it was increasingly difficult to manage in the little cottage. We applied for a council house and were overjoyed when we finally got a place on a housing estate at the other end of town. We were getting ready to move when David, our eldest boy said. 'Jim, I've heard that the people at the new place are not very nice, they said at my school that lots of horrid people live there, and they call it Toe Rag End.'

I hadn't heard anything about what sort of area it was.

'Well,' I said, and smiled. 'We won't worry about them son! Sure, when we lived in Ireland, we had pigs living in a pigsty next to us, they can't be worse than that, can they?'

He didn't reply, but shrugged and looked sideways at the floor.

June was still keen on fostering and although we had been turned down, she felt she would pursue this line. Shortly after we moved, she told me she had phoned Social Services, with regard to fostering.

'Here we go again,' I thought, 'For goodness' sake we were rejected when we had three kids, we've now got six!'

'How did you find out about these Social Services and their fostering; who recommended them?'

She smiled. 'No one, I just picked the phone up, and asked for a Social services number, and that was the one I got, so I phoned them, and someone is coming out to see us with regard to fostering.'

I had to work that day, so the visit was to be with June and the smaller children who were not yet of school age; the others were all at school. This time the social worker was a lady, and as it was a beautiful day, June took them up to the common for the afternoon. The lady was lovely, and she was quite taken with June and the kids. She took up references and arranged another visit. So, as it was called back then, we were 'vetted,' and accepted as Foster Carers.

Armed with the experience of having six children of our own; five boys and a girl, we thought we were ready for anything, but in the days that followed, very quickly learned that we were anything but ready!

First Placement.

'They're bringing a fifteen-year-old boy later on today; they say he works at a low level,' June said excitedly.

We really didn't see anything odd when he arrived with three social workers. We naturally assumed that was how they went about things. It wasn't until we had been fostering for some time that we realised that most children came with a Social Worker, not three!

'This is Norman,' they said, 'He will have to go to the Doctors as he has a little problem with his ears.'

He wasn't remotely interested in anything they had to say, and rubbing his hands together excitedly, he said: 'Dracula's on tonight misses, it's the late-night horror movie; can I watch it?'

'If you're good, I don't see a problem with that,' June said asserting her authority, and turning to the Social Worker in charge, she said: 'I'll take him to the Doctor's in a little while.'

Back then, the setting of restrictions on film categories wasn't adhered to as strictly as it is today, and the social workers didn't pick that up either.

At the surgery, there were quite a few middle-class mothers sitting in silence with their children in the packed waiting room. Norman leaned around one mother, and sniffed loudly, then said to her little girl who was around ten years old: 'Are you gonna watch the late-night horror movie tonight love? It's Dracula.'

The lady, nostrils flaring, glared at him and wrapped her arms protectively around her little girl, turned her back on him, and jerked her head upwards as though disgusted, but didn't speak. June went scarlet and tugged his sleeve.

'Shush!' She said, 'If you don't be quiet, you won't be watching anything!'

Shuffling up and down in his chair, he scowled at June. A little man with glasses leaned round the door and called: 'Next please!'

'Who's that?' Norman enquired.

June, smiled and nodded approval, 'That's our Doctor, Doctor Wilson.'

Norman sniffed loudly again, 'Well, I'm not going in there to see that fucking squinty eyed bastard!'

June, shocked, said: 'If you don't sit there and be quiet, you will not be watching any movie, tonight or any other night!'

The rest of the waiting period passed without further incident. The Doctor advised her to get him some earplugs; grommets, that he needed for swimming. According to the Social workers, he was a very good swimmer.

As time went by, we felt that Norman was Foetal Alcohol Syndrome. His behaviour was like that of a permanent drunk. Later on, we learned that he had been living alone with his alcoholic mother, but she died of liver failure, and that was the reason he was in care.

Where we lived, about five metres in front of our house, by the side of the main road, there was a three-foot wall, with a ten-foot drop on the other side. Norman spent the second day leaning on the wall, spitting on the passers-by walking below. June was not quite ready for this, but managed to get through the day.

June thought it would be a good idea to send him off swimming! It didn't matter that David, our eldest boy, was slightly younger than him, sure David could take them all, it would give her a break, and do them good. There would be no problem, David was an excellent swimmer and the pool catered for small children.

June gave Norman his money separately, and gave David money for him and the children, and sent them on their way all kitted out. Upon arrival, although David protested, Norman was adamant and said: 'I'm not paying good money to go into that shit hole!'

David said, 'Mum told me we were to stick together, and I was to take the kids in, so we have to go in!'

He left Norman to follow, paid for the children and they went in. To his amazement, when they got inside, Norman was already in, and had his trunks on. Grinning at David, he laughed and said: 'Ha! I jumped over the wall.'

When in the water, they said: 'Norman could swim like a fish.'

As usual, at holiday time, the pool was crowded with children; Norman was probably the oldest one there. Every time he got close to young girls in the pool, he dived under and they shrieked and looked really startled, and he emerged from the water laughing; he thought it was a big joke.

One of the girls fetched the attendant. 'That's him,' she said, pointing at him.

'Yes, that's him,' another girl joined in: 'He grabbed me too.'

The attendant pointed at Norman and shouted: 'Right, you! Out of the pool!'

Norman stuck his middle finger up: 'Bollocks,' he laughed and swam to the other side.

'Get him!' The attendant shouted to his colleague, and he dived in, in pursuit. This rapidly developed into something of a Charlie Chaplin chase. Norman swam across the pool, jumped out, ran round and dived back in and then did the same again. Although the attendants were expert swimmers, he managed to elude them for some time.

Finally, they caught him, and he protested his innocence. 'I didn't do naffink and if you're chucking me out, I want my money back!'

'You will get a full refund,' the attendant told him: 'But you will not be allowed back in; you are barred for life!'

David rounded the children up and took them out. Norman laughed all the way home at how he got his money back when he hadn't paid in the first place.

June had a go about his behaviour, and he refused to eat his dinner, called her a hook-nosed jelly-assed bitch and stormed off, outside. He spent a good part of the rest of the day telling passers-by: 'That's my Foster Mother in there, she's a hook-nosed jelly-assed bitch and she needn't think I'm going in to eat the shit she dishes up for dinner.'

Much later, he came in and as though nothing had happened, in a really soft voice he asked, 'What's for dinner misses?'

June was so exasperated that she said, 'Exactly what you've been telling everyone!'

The next day Trevor came running: 'Mummy, Mummy! Norman is sitting on the wall up by the old people's home shouting a load of swear words, and a crowd has gathered round him.'

'Well, I'm certainly not going up there to be another face in the crowd,' she said, 'someone will probably call the police and they will have to deal with it!'

Trevor went back and Norman was still giving out a non-stop stream of expletives. A little old man with glasses, looking as though he'd had enough, was standing nearby with arms akimbo. he pushed his glasses firmly onto the bridge of his nose with his index finger, and marched assertively up to him, wagged his finger at him, and said sternly: 'Look here young man, if you don't stop this nonsense, I shall call the police!'

Norman said: 'Shut up! You fucking old squinty eyed bastard!'

The old man couldn't believe his ears and glanced at Trevor. Trevor shrugged and tapped his temple with his index finger.

'Nuts! He certainly is! Yes, he's nuts!' The old man said tapping his temple, then he spun around and walked away.

Norman laughed and hopped down off the wall, then walked off through the crowd as though nothing had happened. He went straight back to the house and Trevor, with his hand over his mouth, walked around ten paces behind him, sniggering.

I would say we were thrown in at the deep end; we had no idea that people like Norman existed. We had a couple of hectic weeks with him, after which they sent us written instructions, saying that we had to take him to Euston station at 2.30pm on the Saturday. He would be going to Wales, on holiday with a group of teenagers.

When she showed me the note, I smirked and said, 'He'll drive them crackers, won't he?' She shrugged.

I had to work that morning, so June said she would take him on the train. I managed to get off early and rushed home intending to take them in the car. As I approached the house, I could hear him shouting, 'I'm not going on no fucking train!'

I entered the living room, and June dropped her hands by her sides and sighed: 'He's been going on like this all morning.'

He was about three feet out from the corner, sitting on a stool with his back to everyone.

'Don't worry love,' I said, 'I'll take him in the car.'

He sprang off the stool, and facing us, shouted furiously, 'I'm not getting in no fucking car!'

June, put her arms out, appealing to him: 'But Norman, they've told us to take you to Euston.'

He shouted it again and as she moved towards him, he went berserk, swinging his arms wildly, then he kicked the stool and it shot across the room. As he went charging around the room, the phone rang and I grabbed it. 'Yes?' I snapped impatiently.

A tiny female voice said, 'We have been waiting for Norman, and he's not here yet, I just wondered if anything had happened to him.'

'What? He's not supposed to be there until two thirty, it's only just gone eleven.'

'Oh, no!' She said urgently. 'I don't know who told you that, that's wrong! Eleven thirty, that's the time he is supposed to be here, eleven thirty! We can wait for him until twelve o'clock but then I'm afraid we shall have to leave without him, or we will miss all our connections!'

I put my hand over the mouthpiece and shouted, 'June!'

Everything stopped and there was a moment of silence. She looked at me in surprise and I pointed at Norman: 'He is supposed to be at Euston at half eleven, they say they can wait until twelve, but then they'll have to leave without him.'

'I'm not getting in no fucking car,' he screamed and ran out of the room.

June brought her hands to her cheeks. 'Oh my God! He has to go! I couldn't stand another two weeks of this.'

I took my hand off the mouthpiece and shouted: 'He'll be there!'

I slammed the phone down and went into the hall after them. He was still shouting and flailing his arms, slapping her about her arms and shoulders, and hurting her. I took hold of her and ushered her behind me, then grabbed him by his shirtfront: 'Get in the car!' I growled.

He was certain I was going to hit him. 'Yes! Yes! Yes!' He shouted and brought his hands up to protect his face, then he ran outside to get in the car. We ushered the children outside as quickly as we could, and as I was about to move off, he murmured, 'I haven't got any shoes on.'

Everyone laughed and it eased the atmosphere; Trevor ran and fetched them for him. We arrived at Euston, and the coach, about to leave, was ticking over with blue smoke drifting from the exhaust. The young woman, with one foot on the steps about to board, was waiting impatiently. I grabbed his bag and we ran, and the girl stood aside as he boarded.

'I thought he wasn't coming,' she said, 'I'm afraid we have to leave straight away.'

She went up the steps and they folded away, and as the doors closed, the coach moved off.

I thought we would never see him again. The powers that be said that he was 'un-fosterable,' and I had to agree. As we were novices in all of this, it made me wonder why they had brought him in the first place.

Quite some time later, June said that they asked if we would visit him. He had ended up in a special unit along with other disturbed children. June said she thought that would be nice, so reluctantly, I agreed.

It was a beautiful day and I had the windows in our mini-bus wound down. We pulled up in the rather grand car park, and a young boy, with his hands deep in his pockets, strutted over to us in a belligerent manner, and I glanced at him as I took the key out of the ignition.

He sniffed loudly, and sticking his chin out, he said: 'Who have you come to see then mate?'

'Norman Mooney.' I said.

'Ha ha, ha!' He laughed and ran off shouting: 'They've come to see Mooney the looney!'

I glanced at June and she bit her lip.

Later on, we did have him for a couple of weekends and visited him at different places. One of these was another special secure unit that housed a lot of disturbed young teenage boys and girls. We were ushered through a steel door, and it was locked behind us; security was paramount! We were about to sit down, and Norman grabbed June's arm and shouted urgently: 'Ah! Don't sit in that chair, that's where they all have it off!'

She came out of it as though it was on fire.

Later on, we even visited him in Hospital when he was being dried out.

The Council gave him a flat of his own, and sometimes we took him out for a meal. On one occasion, he phoned us and stormed, 'The pigs have raided my place for drugs - twice! And you know I don't have anything to do with any of that shit! Bastards!'

I thought perhaps that was true. Alcohol had always been his problem. I wondered, 'Poor Norman, what chance does he have in life?'

Glen and Erica.

With the coming and going of social workers, we could feel hostility building up among the neighbours. I think they were of the opinion that we were having dealings with Social Services and planning to remove their children.

A short period elapsed and we were asked to look after Glen and Erica, two siblings; an eight-year-old boy, and a three-year-old girl. Both children were highly disturbed. I came home one evening, and June was standing by the kitchen window, looking out onto the garden. I went and stood by her side.

Without turning round, she asked: 'Would you call that creative play?'

I couldn't believe my eyes. Glen and the smaller children had virtually demolished everything in the garden that I had spent months trying to make look nice. They had made a pyramid of everything, including my gardening and work tools. Each one had a tool of some description, and using them like axes, had completely destroyed the new lawn.

'Damn it!' I exclaimed. 'I'll give them creative play; I'll wring their necks!' I dashed out of the door and up the garden steps, and holding my hands aloft I yelled, 'Stop!'

They all stopped in their tracks, and Peter, diffusing the situation, said in his chirpy little voice, 'Hello Jim!'

June's voice came from the kitchen window, 'They had all better come in now anyway, their tea is ready.'

They washed their hands and settled at the table. It had been a bit of an ordeal since these kids arrived, their table manners were abominable, and of course our kids thought that was great fun. The effort we had put in trying to teach our kids etiquette was being demolished. This went on for quite some time until David suddenly said, 'We don't think that's funny; we think it's rude!'

The others chimed in, 'Yuk, it's rude!'

June was serving the meals and I was taking them to the table.

'Did you hear that?' I whispered, and she smiled and nodded.

From that time on there was a really big improvement in them. Erica even stopped filling her mouth until it bulged, which she had done repeatedly since they arrived. The result being that she dribbled saliva down her front, and it would be whatever colour the food she was eating happened to be at that particular time. The improvements were noticed not only by us, but by everyone, including the school and the congregation at the Church we went to on Sundays. We always had light refreshments after the Service, and a man we had known for some time said he couldn't help but notice the amazing change for the better in our foster children.

'Who do you foster for, would you consider fostering for us?'

He said the name of the Council he represented, and I spluttered into my tea and pointed at June: 'You'd better ask her! She might not fancy that idea, your authority rejected us a few years ago.'

He said he was their Foster and Adoptions Officer, and was not very happy at the news we had just given him.

Social Services decided that Glen and Erica should go back to their mother, a very needy girl who had a change of live-in boyfriends on a regular basis. While her children were with us, we had her stay overnight on numerous occasions, when she 'accidentally' missed the last train back home. We felt we knew her fairly well, and I wondered if we were actually fostering her as well.

On the day the decision was to be taken, a meeting was arranged at our house. The headmaster of the children's school, having witnessed what he described as: 'The amazing change in the children,' he felt so strongly against them returning, that he insisted on attending. Despite his protests, the decision was made that they should return. We never saw Glen or Erica again.

Over the years, I have often wondered what becomes of kids we take under our wing during a crisis in their lives, but invariably we never find out. I found that practice extremely odd and thought it could even be damaging. Having been brought up in the care of the really tough children's home that we called 'The School.' While I was there, I hated it, and yearned for the day when I would go home. That day came and it was wonderful; ah, freedom! While I was there, a good many of the 'old boys' after they left, they came back visiting, not just once, but on numerous occasions. At the time, I thought, 'why the hell would anyone want to come back to visit this dump?' I just couldn't understand it, all I wanted to do was to see the back of it, and good riddance! On the day that I was released, I arrived home to a grand welcome. My Mum hugged and kissed me, then smiling, she looked into my face and said: 'Welcome home son, it's so good to know that you don't ever have to go back to that awful place again.'

I looked around my family, they were all clapping, it was the most wonderful day of my life; I loved it!

However, not very long after I left, I yearned to go back, just for a visit, but unfortunately, shortly after I left, 'The School' closed down and moved to a new place that I didn't know. That left a void within me that time would never erase; even now, over seventy years later, the thought of it still pulls at my heart strings.

Many years later on in our fostering, we lived in a large ex-children's home and on a number of occasions, we had grown men in their late thirties and forties, turn up with their family and knock on our door and say: 'You don't know me, but as a child I lived in this children's home. Would it be too much trouble to ask if I could have a look round, please?'

I knew all too well what they were going through, and because of that, I have always felt that secrecy, when foster children, even after years of staying with us, were spirited away never to be seen again, was so wrong; especially for the children. That was the very reason when we adopted our four children, we always had open adoptions, so that the natural parents were able to contact or even visit. We wanted to do our utmost to ensure that we would never obliterate any link, and inflict this feeling of bereavement on the parents, or the children, but I digress.

Jean.

We were in line to adopt Jean, a lovely little red-haired girl the same age as Ellie, our only girl out of six children. She would be coming long term, with a view to adoption. We thought it would be wonderful to have another little girl; a friend for Ellie. A meeting was set up and we were taken by Jean's social worker to visit her current foster carers. They were a very nice couple and made us welcome. The lady was rather glamorous and the man was a very masculine, quite successful businessman. We hit it off really well, and just as we were finishing our tea, Jean's social worker, out of the blue, said: 'What about your family secrets?'

The man, looking puzzled, shook his head and said: 'Family secrets, what family secrets?'

In a rather scornful manner, she said: 'You haven't even told the child that you go to the toilet in a bag.'

He went scarlet, and I was so shocked and thought: 'Good grief, what a vindictive bitch!

Oh my goodness, when Jean arrives, we'll be dealing with her.' I found that prospect more than a little unnerving.

It completely destroyed the meeting, and feeling really embarrassed, we left almost straight away. I couldn't get my head round why she had said it.

Much to my surprise, Jean's placement went without a hitch and she moved in. She became such good friends with Ellie, playing games, and generally getting on so well with each other, and I thought it was wonderful. She had been with us quite a while, and as June and I watched them through the window, they played in the garden. I pointed at Jean and said: 'She's cheating, and she's quite nasty with it.'

June said: 'I know, it's been going on for quite some time now. It really is getting Ellie down, and it's not doing me a lot of good either. I was talking to her the other day and mentioned her cheating, she told me that she didn't care how she beat Ellie, just as long as she beat her. It doesn't matter about anyone else, just Ellie. She is competing with her on every single thing she does.'

She had been with us for a considerable time, and settled in. A thing that we normally did with the kids was; on their birthday, June and I would take just the birthday boy or girl, out for a meal; a special treat on their own.

A few days before we were to take Jean out for her birthday treat, June and I were talking and because I had been in care, in many ways I instinctively knew how these kids think, and I said: 'You know what? If you told Jean you were fed up with her and had to get rid of her, she wouldn't turn a hair.'

'Don't talk ridiculous,' she snapped, so I didn't say any more.

I forgot all about our conversation, and during our meal out with her, June said: 'Jean, if I said to you that we didn't want you anymore and you had to go, would you feel very sad?'

Jean said: 'No, of course not, I'd have to concentrate on the new foster family I'd be going to.'

June looked blankly at me and I shrugged.

As time wore on, Jean was still striving ever more in competition with Ellie, and Ellie being quite athletic, always did well at games, made it very difficult for her. I arrived home from work and June greeted me with a smile. 'Jean came second in the school sports today.'

'Excellent,' I said, 'I bet she's proud of herself then,' and she said, 'You know who came first?' I raised my eyebrows and she said, 'Ellie!'

'Ah well, I suppose that says it all,' I said.

During the period that followed, her jealousy of the other children and her fierce competitiveness towards Ellie grew to unbearable proportions. Ellie withdrew completely and spent most of her time in her room, isolated and alone. Jean turned her attention mainly to Joe which I thought was odd, him being four years younger. On several occasions she 'set him up.' She watched for him coming out of the bathroom, and went in immediately after him and squeezed a whole tube of toothpaste, smeared it everywhere, then emptied a tin of talcum powder all around and said to June, 'Go and look at the state of the bathroom! Joe's just come out of there.'

It was only after a lot of painful accusations and trauma for everyone that she broke down sobbing and said: 'I don't know why I did it.'

But she had already achieved her aim and it didn't end there. I was watching television, and she was on the carpet, playing with Joe. Although she thought I couldn't see her, I was watching her intently out of the corner of my eye. She was sitting astride him, holding him in a wrestling grip with his arms pinned flat on the floor. He was having such a good time, laughing and giggling, and I thought that was so sweet; her playing with little Joe and giving him some attention, contrasting her previous behaviour towards him. She glanced at me several times and I smiled inwardly, thinking, 'perhaps we have turned a corner.'

Suddenly, without warning, she leapt off the floor, and leaving just her hands holding his wrists, she came down full weight with both her knees on his biceps. He shrieked in pain, and as I lunged from my chair, in an effort to stop him wailing, she put her face close to his, and kissed him on the cheek, then patting his face gently, she said, 'Sorry baby, did I hurt you?'

I took her arm and lifted her bodily off him, 'Of course you hurt him!' I growled.

'It was an accident,' she wept; Joe was howling.

As I cuddled and tried to comfort him, she stood in front of me, sobbing into her hands, ostensibly distressed, and she said: 'I didn't mean it, it was an accident.'

'It was no accident,' I said, 'I saw you do it. Don't touch or play with him again, you can't be trusted!'

She had done it and there was nothing I could do about it, and that made me very nervous. In the weeks that followed, her attitude, her behaviour, and constant manipulation became unbearable. Finally, with the aid of our support worker, we decided that this was not going to work, so the decision was made that she would have to be moved on. It was nevertheless psychologically very painful to make the break. There were occasions when we had talks regarding it.

June said: 'If she was our own daughter and behaved this way, we wouldn't get rid of her, would we?'

I said: 'That's the whole problem, it's the fact that she's not ours that makes her behave the way she does. She's so jealous of the other kids, she feels that she is the odd one out, and no matter how long we keep her, or how much we do for her, that will always be a fact of life, that part of her even you can't change!'

I waited but she didn't reply and I continued, 'She seems to think that if she beats Ellie, everyone will think she's just wonderful and we'll all love her.' June nodded silently in agreement.

The day she was to be removed arrived, and we all said our goodbyes, but that was after she had taunted the children, laughing and saying, 'She was moving up!' She got into the back of her social worker's car, and although she had told us that she would have to be thinking of her new foster family, she became very distressed and pressing her face against the window she gave us a final wave. Tears were streaming down her face and she looked as though she was unable to escape the torment. All our children were beside us on the pavement, howling. As the car pulled away, it didn't occur to us that we might never see her again. Even then, I didn't realise that the break would be total. A child, whom you have cared for as your own, just snuffed out. It left us with a feeling of bereavement as would a death. I wondered how she must have felt, any feelings that we or she had, were totally disregarded; just like the men who knocked on our door; the link was broken.

About 12 years later, she got back in touch and came for a visit. She told us she was finished with Social Services and was now out of care. The fact that she initiated the move was nice. Of course, we couldn't have contacted her, we hadn't a clue where she had gone, but because she did, I still think I was right. I thought her time in care had left its mark, she had the air about her of a child in care. I couldn't help thinking how much better she would have been with us, but then, what would the cost have been for us, or more importantly, our children?

Tony and Sophie.

We were placed two little siblings; Tony, about 18 months and his baby sister Sophie, about 9 months. The Social Worker informed us, 'They have both been in Hospital with infectious Hepatitis, but that's all cleared up now, so they're fine.'

When children are placed, it might be because they are thought to be in danger. Quite often, there is no actual proof of abuse, but they are like a window that you can look through and see just what they have suffered or experienced.

Our friend Sally came for a visit, and upon seeing Tony, she scooped him up. 'So, this is Tony, oh, isn't he gorgeous? Just look at those golden curls.' She said, smiling as she studied him.

Her mouth dropped open and her eyes popped when he stuck his hand down the front of her blouse and quite aggressively, fondled her breast.

'Oh my God!' she said, as she put him down. She put her hand to her lips, not knowing whether to smile or not; June was flabbergasted! Sally bit her bottom lip thoughtfully and said: 'It was bad enough him having a good grope, but all the grunting the went with it, that's what I found so shocking. A little child like that, hardly old enough to talk, but heavily into sex orgies -well!'

Tony scuttled off, running around as though nothing had happened. A few days later, on a hot sunny day. Sophie, with only a nappy on, was asleep on the settee, her arms and legs spread-eagle. We were having cold drinks when Tony toddled into the room, climbed onto the settee, and to our amazement, started going through the motions of having sex with her; with full sound effects!

They had been with us a matter of weeks when our five-year old came into our room and clambered onto the bed. I was still half asleep and June's voice roused me. 'Jim, do you think Sammy's eyes look a bit yellow?'

I sat bolt upright and gasped. 'What? 'Oh God, they are, what the hell are we going to do?'

'Get the Doctor I suppose,' she said calmly.

I said: 'Hepatitis is deadly you know.'

The doctor arrived and sure enough, he had Hepatitis. The doctor looked around and said, 'this is very serious, you will all have to be inoculated and quarantined.'

The children were delighted, 'Yippee, no school!'

June said: 'We'll keep them off however long it takes!'

He then said: 'I'm afraid it means no play as well, at least not with other children.' He nodded at me and said: 'That also applies to you too! You won't be able to go to work either! You will all have to cut yourselves off from outside contact until you are considered to be cleared!'

I told him I was working in a derelict house and had no need to leave it as all the materials were on site.

He said: 'In that case I should think it is alright, you could carry on.'

'Thank goodness for that,' I said, 'We can't afford to be quarantined, we have a hard-enough time making ends meet, even when I am working.'

As he was leaving, he said: 'We could have an epidemic on our hands and we don't want that, do we?'

I said, 'Well! This is a fine mess, isn't it? How are we going to get our groceries?'

'He said we could get most of them delivered,' she replied.

The news spread like wildfire and the phone went non-stop.

One lady, another foster carer phoned and said: 'I think this is terrible, somebody has to take responsibility for this! You are not alone you know, the lady who took those children on emergency placement for one night before they came to you, has also contracted hepatitis and she is extremely ill with it. It's very severe on adults, especially women.'

'Good God!' I said in exasperation, 'She's cheered me up no end, it sounds like the plague.'

A shadow passed the window and there was a light knock on the back-kitchen door.

'There's somebody at the door,' June said, 'you'll have to get rid of them.'

By the time I got to the kitchen, Gordon, the odd chap from next door was already inside. His wife had also died of liver failure, and fearing social services would take his little girl, we had fostered her, so, he was a regular visitor and, in the meantime, he was helping me at the derelict house. I tapped my forehead with the heel of my hand, as though jolting my memory. 'Damn it Gordon,' I said. 'I clean forgot you were coming round today. I'm afraid you can't stay; we've got infectious Hepatitis in the house and we are all under quarantine!'

'Pah!' He said, dismissing it with a wave of his hand. 'Hepatitis? I don't give a damn about that; what about a cup of tea?'

He moved past me and filled the kettle. June had followed me in, and I looked at her and shrugged. She smiled and I could see her shoulders jerking up and down, as she laughed silently to herself.

Moving up.

We came through the quarantine and later moved to a five-bedroom house set on the edge of a rather nice estate, and as we were the end of terrace, we had a large playing field next to and in front of us; perfect for the children.

We were asked if we could take a little Down syndrome girl. Megan was not a year old yet, and was to be placed with us for adoption. June had seen her on several occasions and thought she was lovely. The thing that I found strange was, social services wanted an answer before I had even seen her. although apprehensive, I reluctantly agreed. A meeting was arranged to bring her to the house. Having six children was very demanding, so my work schedule was, busy, busy, busy, anyway, I skipped work that day; a rare event.

June was very excited, looking forward to seeing her again, and with her enthusiasm, had me quite keen too. I knew what to expect, after all, hadn't we had Sophie, a bonny bouncing little girl a little while ago?

The Social worker arrived and June, smiled as she ushered her with Megan, into the garden where I was sitting in the sun, and we said hello. June was right, Megan was lovely, and I knew I had done the right thing in agreeing, all my doubts were erased. We were chatting happily and having tea, when June stood up and took Megan from the Social Worker.

'Here, let Jim hold her!' She said.

I smiled and held my arms out. The shock on my face was secondary to the sharp intake of breath that plainly said I was alarmed.

'What's wrong?' They said in unison; I shook my head in silence.

'Give her to me.' June said, and took her. 'What's wrong?' She repeated.

'Is she alright?' I said softly, 'she feels so - limp.'

'Oh, is that all?' June said, 'that's quite normal, a lot of Down syndrome babies have no muscle tone, or very little.'

'Well... nobody told me and I don't have to tell you, I was shocked.' I was still shaking my head.

'I understand his reaction,' the social worker said.

June said: 'I suppose he was expecting a cuddly little baby like Sophie.'

'What's going to happen then?' The Social worker enquired, looking from June to me.

I asked, 'Are there any books or leaflets on this condition?'

'I'm sure we can get in touch with someone who can give us all the information we require,' the social worker said more to June than me.

She left, and June tried to give me reassurance. 'It doesn't matter! How you reacted is of no consequence.'

'I was just not prepared,' I said. 'I'm sorry, it was such a shock, she felt so limp and floppy. I got the feeling that she would not be long for this world, I don't know what I felt really.'

Before she left, the social worker assured us that she would forward any relevant information regarding Megan's condition, and I thought, not knowing, that was a must, because without any information, I just could not proceed.

It was quite nice occasionally to all get in the mini-bus and go over to our old Church. June and the children loved it, and even I enjoyed it, so we went the following Sunday.

After the service, everyone was having tea and chatting. We ended up talking to the Minister, and June mentioned the setback we'd had with Megan.

'It's a terrible thing,' he said. 'Young David and his wife,' he pointed to familiar faces across the hall. 'Their new baby is Down syndrome, perhaps you should have a word with them, in fact here they are now.'

'Hello.' They smiled as they approached. 'How do you like your new place then?'

'We haven't really settled in yet,' June said. 'So, it's a bit early to say, it seems okay though.'

We explained our situation. This was a time when there were no computers or internet, and because of my work schedule, I couldn't take time off to go hunting for literature.

'Are there any books, or leaflets...?' We gave him our new address and he said he would send us whatever he had or could get hold of. I felt relieved knowing that I would at least have the answer to any queries I might have. I watched for the post every day and at the end of two weeks, I was certain that nothing was coming. Nothing from David and nothing from the Social

Worker. I told June that I felt unable to proceed with Megan, and she was very understanding. She said: 'If that's how you feel, I won't try to persuade you one way or the other.'

We informed social services of our decision so that they could make alternative arrangements. We heard through the grapevine that Megan went to a family in the Midlands, some considerable distance away, but we learned shortly after that sadly, it had broken down.

We carried on with our lives and it wasn't long before the summer holidays arrived. My work was at a stage where it was impossible to knock off for the beginning of the school holidays. June very bravely decided to take the children to the camping site in Somerset. I would drop them off, stay for the weekend, then I would have to return and carry on working.

'I'll be alright,' she assured me. 'I'll be on the same site as the other Foster Parents.'

We had met a group of Foster Parents a couple of years earlier, and they had a complete section of the camp site set aside purely for that purpose; foster families only. Surprisingly some of them lived just a few miles from us. It seemed odd, living just around the corner and being introduced a hundred and sixty miles away.

Under the circumstances, I thought that June and the kids would be okay. So, I was happy to take them and set everything up.

A few days before we were due to leave, a social worker we didn't know phoned and said: 'Would you be able to take a disturbed teenager for two weeks?'

June replied, 'We can't! We are going camping in a few days.'

'Well, can you not take him with you?'

'I think you had better tell me about him,' June said.

When the Social Worker paid us a visit; she said that she had tried everywhere to place Terry. If we couldn't take him, he would be going to a secure unit in Northampton, a place mainly for disturbed children; that was the choice, there was just nothing else for him. He had a history of running, hence the secure unit. It all seemed really dreadful, especially when we recalled the so-called 'Special unit' where we had visited Norman.

The social worker said: 'He has a few problems.'

June said: 'Like what?'

'Em, he's a soiler, and he's also into glue sniffing. He's over six feet tall, he's a skinhead, he has been known to be violent – and, he's a runner!'

'Sounds charming,' June said.

Despite his record, June felt that she would give him a chance; provided the children didn't object too strongly. They listened to his list of 'attributes,' and Joe piped up, 'Yes, but does he smoke?'

'Yes, he does,' she said.

'Yeough!' Joe said, turning his top lip up and crinkling his nose as though there was a nasty smell under it. 'Well, he'll have to smoke outside in the garden then.'

June nodded, 'Yes and why not?'

So, that was it, he was coming with us. When he arrived, we wondered if we weren't off our trolleys agreeing to take him. His hair was less than a quarter of an inch long, psychedelic blue (unheard of in those days) and he had Doctor Martin boots with about eighteen lace holes, black skin-tight jeans tucked in, and large safety pins in his ears serving as earrings; he just oozed aggression. Still, we had agreed so we were determined to see it through. During the course of the two weeks, he presented no problems. June even managed to penetrate his armour and had quite a few heart-to-hearts with him, and he confided in her. He had been in care from six weeks old, two siblings; him and an older brother. Their sister had been placed for adoption straight away, so they had lost contact with her. His older brother was now living in his own flat and holding down a job. His deprived background had not affected him as badly as Terry's. They never put him forward for fostering or adoption which we thought was odd. He was moved to a children's home where he stayed until he was fourteen, the age at which they move them out from that particular children's home to another 'unit.' He promptly ran away and disappeared for six weeks. Everyone was amazed how he managed to survive on the run for such a long time. From the talks they were having, June knew that he was highly intelligent and extremely resourceful.

'Where on earth did you go?'

He said: 'I did a few burglaries to get money for food, then I went back to my old children's home.'

'I'm surprised they let you stay.'

He laughed. 'They didn't, the kids knew I was there but the staff had no idea. I hid in the loft and the kids fed me. I used to come out at nights to wash and go to the toilet.'

'Six weeks? So, what happened then?'

'When they found me, they took me back to the new place, I hated it. The decision was made that I would be put in a secure unit, you know, a lock up? Two social workers who knew me while I had been in the old place, were so disgusted with the decision to lock me up, they smuggled me out and hid me. They said that they wouldn't let anyone know where I was until some alternative was arranged.'

'And was some alternative arranged?'

'Well, I'm here now, ain't I? And I ain't going to no fuckin' lock up!'

When they arrived home, the two weeks had been a very agreeable period for Terry. He had found his long-lost foster family and he wasn't going to let this chance slip by. We were lumbered with him, whether we liked it or not!

David was working with me on a painting job, so I said I would take Terry along to give June a break. I showed Terry how to rub down a few wood window frames, ready for painting. I thought he had very little concentration, and after a very short period he was back. 'I've done that, what'll I do now?'

'He can't possibly have done it,' I thought.

'Right, let's go and have a look.' To my amazement they were done, and quite well too. I set him another task and within a very short time we had the same performance. This happened a few times. He just didn't seem to have the interest in order to be able to carry out the work the way he was doing it.

I went to see how David was. 'How are you getting on then mate?' I said.

I could see at a glance he wasn't doing too well; certainly not up to his usual standard.

'Not very well to be honest,' he said. 'That boy keeps coming to me and saying, 'I'm fed up doing this, can you do it?' So, I've really been doing his work.'

So that he wouldn't be able to skive off, I took him with me to do a flat roof, and to my surprise, he did very well.

A few months elapsed, each with its own little incidents, and we were into late autumn. Terry was with a crowd of kids, outside at the door. The laughter and very boisterous behaviour reached a pitch that I thought I had better intervene. As I entered the hall, the half-glass front door burst open, and Terry ran in with Ellie hot on his heels. Laughing, he slammed the door to prevent her from catching him. Instinctively, she put her hands up to stop it slamming in her face. Her hands smashed the obscure glass and went through the gap. With no glass in the door, she was clearly visible, and I could see the shocked expression on her face.

'Terry!' She shouted in disgust.

To my horror, a large scallop of flesh, the shape and almost the size of a flat lemon, was hanging from the underside of her forearm. After the initial shock, the pain registered and she looked to see what it was and staggering back in alarm, she shrieked in panic.

I shouted at one of the children: 'Quick! get me a towel!' And as he dashed up the stairs, I shouted again, 'A clean one!'

Surprisingly, there was very little blood as it was such a clean slice. I tried not to look as though I was rushing as I took her hand and gently wrapped the towel around the wound, making sure the section of flesh was in place. I ushered her to the car and sped off to the hospital. She had to have over fifty stitches and when we returned, Terry was sitting with his head in his hands, sobbing.

She said, 'You needn't sit there grizzling Terry! It was an accident and it can't be helped.'

Over the months that followed, the wound rejected the section of flesh, and she was left with a permanent scar, plus an indent almost the size of a palm print.

Christmas was just around the corner and I thought it would be nice if we got some cocktail mixers in. Although we didn't drink, they were especially nice if we had visitors. I got rum and Coke, Cinzano and lemonade, Advocaat for snowballs, wine, sherry, whiskey, lager and a few others. I put them in the cabinet for safe keeping, and never gave them another thought. June and I were invited out to supper about a week before Christmas, and David assured us that he was perfectly capable of looking after the children. After all, he was now coming sixteen; just how old did he have to be to qualify as a babysitter? Feeling assured, we set off to enjoy our evening out. Upon our return, David was in a rather hyped-up state.

June asked, 'What on earth has happened here?'

'Terry's gone!' He said, 'I gave him a smack in the gob. He was absolutely blotto, and I found him trying to force a bottle of Rum down Peter's throat. He was sitting on Peter's bed, and I wouldn't have known he was there except, as I was passing the door, I heard him say, 'C'mon Peter, get this down you!' Peter started spluttering and coughing and I dashed in. When I saw what he was doing, I smacked him one. We had a sort of a scuffle and he ran out of the door, that was over an hour ago.'

I asked, 'What about Peter, is he alright?'

We rushed up to Peter's room, he was only nine years old, and sleeping peacefully.

David said, 'I don't think he swallowed much of it, he was asleep at the time and coughed it up. I cleaned him up and he went back to sleep.'

When we had a look, not just some of our Christmas drinks, but all of them were gone!

I said, 'God! He's a stupid sod! It's a good job David was able to deal with him, otherwise, goodness knows what would have happened. He's lucky he hasn't got alcoholic poisoning with that amount of drink.'

June raised her eyebrows, 'That's right, I wonder where he is now?'

'I don't know, and at the moment, I don't much care either,' I retorted.

'Does this whole episode not tell you anything?' She said, shaking her head.

'Like what?'

'It says that his needs have never been met, he has no idea how to behave in a family environment. Outside influences like drugs, be it alcohol or whatever, just tip him over the edge and he ends up in a situation like this, where he has to run away; that's why they call him a runner.'

She had a very valid point and the more I thought about it, I had to agree that he'd had the rough end of the stick during his life. Even after all this, despite his reckless spells, I still thought that he had potential, so we waited to see what materialised.

Being his Foster Parents and responsible for him, we had to report what happened to Social Services, and inform the police that he was missing. It would be just a matter of time before he would be picked up. As time went by, we felt less irritated about the incident and decided that we would carry on if he did return. He was brought back a couple of weeks later. His manner changed, and he was rather sheepish by comparison with his previous behaviour. We thought that the best course of action would be to keep him occupied as much as possible, so I took him to work with me again; when I had work that was suitable. Going to work with me every now and again helped him financially and as soon as he got a little bit of money, he set his sights on the old CZ motorcycle that I had bought for the kids for dirt tracking. It was fully functional and he kept bartering with David. He was so persistent that in the end David let him have it and he spent all his spare time 'suping' it up, as he called it. He said he was going to make it lighter by taking all the rubbish off it.

I returned from work and June said: 'Terry's in the garden and he has the motorbike in smithereens.'

I opened the French-doors to have a look. Numerous parts were littered on the path all around him. He looked up and said: 'Have you got a spare petrol cap for this?'

I glanced at the heap of bits, 'There is one for it.'

'Yeah, I know, but I've lost it, would cling-film do?'

'Phew! Sounds a bit hairy to me,' I said and went back indoors. I forgot all about it and he never mentioned it again.

About a week later, I came home from work and June, looking exasperated, put her hands to each side of her face and said, 'We've had the Police up here today! That damned bike! He took it over the playing field without a silencer and the racket was absolute purgatory. Someone, or perhaps everyone phoned the police.'

'Did they confiscate the bike?'

She shook her head and gave a mirthless laugh, 'No! They hid in the bushes and the minute he set foot on the parking lot, sprang out and gave him a ticket to produce his documents.'

'That's a bloody joke,' I laughed.

It ran out of petrol and walking with it on his way back to the house, he went off the grass and they sprang out, 'You're nicked,' they sneered and went over the bike with a fine-tooth comb.

It made me wonder, 'Whatever happened to the old Bobby who, when a kid was being a pest, used to either give him a clip round the ear, or put his thumbs in the breast pockets of his tunic, rock back on his heels and say, 'Okay son, you've had your fun, put it away, because next time you'll be in big trouble!'

We had never had contact with the police over our children and way they went about their business didn't exactly fit in with my train of thought.

He wasn't able to produce any documents, so they pressed charges and we went with him on his day in court. I reckoned that he would more than likely be fined a nominal sum and told him I could take him to work with me to cover it. I assured the court that he worked well and I was certain that he would not be a problem in future if they could excuse his irresponsible behaviour this time. I was told to step down from the witness box and the judges had a brief consultation, then one of them addressed Terry.

'Right! I'm going to be lenient with you, I'm not going to send you to prison!'

In shock, I heard the word 'Prison' in my mind; 'prison? For an old motor bike - on a field?'

'I've decided to give you a chance,' he continued. 'Instead, I'm going to fine you the sum of eighty pounds.'

'There you go!' I thought.

I was jolted back to reality when he shuffled some papers in front of him and said, 'On each of the following counts!' He started reeling them off.

'No road fund licence, no M.O.T. no insurance, no crash helmet.'

'Where is he going to get the money?' I uttered aloud.

'Silence!' He roared and pounded the bench with the palm of his hand. 'I haven't finished yet!'

Easing forward in his huge seat, he pointed an accusing finger at Terry and said, 'No lights, defective brakes, defective tyres, no petrol cap, no number plate, no driving licence, no foot rests and no silencer.'

This was a fifteen-year-old boy in care, with no income! I could not comprehend it.

'That's getting on for a thousand pounds,' I whispered to June. 'Where's he going to get the money?'

She didn't answer but looked at the floor and shook her head.

They gave him time to pay so I took him to work with me as often as possible and he paid his fine - for a few weeks.

Six weeks or so later, on a sunny afternoon, he turned up at the house in a car and June said: 'He's driven that car over ten miles to here and God knows what would have happened if he ran into someone.'

I said, 'He doesn't learn, does he? Where is he now?'

'Oh, he's outside with his car; where else?'

I went to have a look; no Terry and no car! One of the children came running and holding his knees with his hands in an effort to regain his breath, he gasped, 'Terry has crashed his car along by the school.'

We rushed to the scene in my van. His car was half way up the pavement, with the front end rammed in the hedge. The driver's door was wide open and our children's baseball bat was sitting on the front passenger seat. On the pavement opposite, lodged against a lamppost with steam billowing from under the bonnet, was a newish car and the driver was studying the damage.

'What's happened here?' I enquired.

He pointed angrily at Terry's car and said, 'This... bastard came careering out of there at me.' He pointed at the road we had just come down. 'He forced me off the road and I mounted the kerb and hit this bloody lamp post.'

'Where is he now then?'

He pointed at a clump of trees, 'I don't know, he ran off through those bushes.'

Terry returned home and his car returned to the car park.

The children told him I had been a mechanic and he asked if I would have a look at it. We went outside and I said: 'Lift the bonnet! Has it got an M.O.T?'

He shook his head and I peered inside at the engine.

'See all this oil on the underside of the bonnet?' I said, pointing at the thick black layer coated inside.

'Uh huh.'

'Well, that probably means that the pistons and rings are worn and it's got compression in the sump. That's why it's blowing it out and everything is plastered in oil. It smokes when it's running, doesn't it?'

He nodded.

I walked around the car and checked the wheels. 'It needs a hundred-quid's worth of tyres, they're all past the limit.'

I squatted and took hold of the top of the front wheel and shook it. 'Hear that knocking?' I said and he nodded. 'Steering's shot to hell.'

I shook the wheel from side to side, more knocking and I glanced at the sky, 'track rod ends are gone as well.' I looked underneath and said: 'At least the bodywork looks sound. Oh! The back nearside wheel is very wet on the inside, that'll be either brakes, or the oil seal!'

I went to the front, looked at him and shook my head. 'Quite honestly Terry, this thing is about ready for the scrap heap. You should have asked me to have a look before embarking on a venture like this.'

I went back into the house and thought no more about it. Upon my arrival home from work the following day, I was amazed. Someone had vandalised Terry's car, there was not a square inch of it that had not been bashed in with bricks or something of that nature. The interior was in tatters and glass from the shattered windows was strewn all around and inside it.

'Who could have done such a thing?' I wondered. 'I wouldn't be surprised if it was the guy who crashed his car. Probably saw it, recognised it and... well, the rest is history.'

June was in the kitchen and I said, 'You should see the state of Terry's car.'

She nodded knowingly. 'Yes, I know, he spent the entire day pounding it with the children's baseball bat; I really think he doesn't love it anymore.'

I put my hand to my mouth and thought for a moment. 'So, it was Terry then?'

'Of course, who else?'

'I thought it might have been the guy who crashed his car the other day.'

She was shaking her head, 'It was Terry!'

'Perhaps I was a bit severe in my assessment of it yesterday.' I said, trying not to smile.

She said, 'Who knows what his reasons are, but I should think that had something to do with it.'

During the weeks that followed, I hadn't sufficient or suitable work to ensure him some sort of income so that he could pay his fines, so I started giving him simple chores at home. The sliding cupboard doors in our little caravan were a bit of an eyesore. What a good idea it would be to get him to cover them? He was quite capable of doing things like this, in fact he was fairly good at precision work, so I bought some rather nice leather and showed him how to stick the first piece on and watched as he did the second one.

'Excellent!' I said, smiling at the result. I felt quite confident leaving him to it. When I arrived home that evening, I glanced into the caravan to see how he had got on. My smile vanished and my mouth dropped open, 'Unbelievable,' I thought. The lines on the first two were perfectly upright. The lines on the third one was at about 1 o'clock and continued in this manner until the last one was just a little off three o'clock.

June was sipping coffee as I entered the room. 'You should see the mess Terry's made of the caravan,' I said, 'Not only are the door coverings crooked, but the cutting on them is absolutely potty as well.'

June nodded knowingly.

'What?' I said as I spread my hands and shook my head.

'Well, Terry was really high on something today.' She said.

I grimaced, looked at the floor, closed my eyes and put my hand to my mouth. 'Of course, Evo-stick! They said he was into glue sniffing; it never entered my head.'

I sat down and gave a little sigh, looked at her and started laughing. She was standing right in front of me. I leaned my head on her midriff and said: 'we can't say too much about that, can we?'

She was laughing and said, 'The less said the better!'

On Friday nights, June usually took the children to a little youth club and decided to take Terry along. It didn't matter if he looked the odd man out with his skinhead appearance, she was sure he would enjoy it. After a few visits, we were informed that the place had been broken into, very badly smashed up and excrement smeared everywhere. Whoever did it, wrote on the wall in blue aerosol spray-paint, 'Skins rule okay!' There were no skinheads where we lived, it was an inner London trait; Terry was the only one!

As the weeks went by, he made no secret of the fact that he wasn't paying his fines. I thought he was heading for trouble, even though I sympathised with him on that score.

It was early evening and having arrived home from work, I was just going in the garden gate to the back door. Three Police vehicles roared in rapid succession into the parking lot alongside of our house. A gang of police emerged, some with dogs and I wondered what that was all about. I carried on, into the living room and before I could tell June what was happening, there was loud pounding on the front door. They didn't ring the bell, or knock, as any normal person would, but pounded in an aggressive manner, presumably with the side of their fist. Upon opening the door, June was confronted by two Policemen, and a Policewoman at the end of the garden path with a colleague, was carrying on a conversation on a walkie-talkie. Others with Police dogs were already patrolling the field.

'We have a warrant for the arrest of Terrance Sayer,' the first policeman growled.

June's mouth dropped open, 'Would you like to come in please?' She said: 'He's not here at the moment.'

As they came in, the others moved off onto the playing field where she thought Terry was. She could feel panic rising, 'What's he being arrested for?'

'Non-payment of fines!' He snapped in a hostile manner. 'Where is he? Is he about?'

June, momentarily lost for words, sank into a chair and sat staring into space.

'My colleagues are looking for him right now, and if he doesn't stand still, he will be savaged by the dogs,' he said menacingly.

This mental picture was just too much for her. She sank back in the chair and broke down in tears. The policeman looked disgustedly at his colleague and glanced at the ceiling.

'You listen to me Mrs Sayer!' He snarled in threatening tones, 'if you are concealing his whereabouts, you will find yourself in very serious trouble!'

Looking rather surprised, she glanced up, 'My name's not Sayer; it's Crowe.'

Clearly puzzled, he shook his head, 'So you're not his mother then?'

'No, I'm his Foster Mother.'

His whole attitude changed, he became very understanding and concerned. 'Oh, I see!' He said in a shocked tone of voice. 'I just don't know how you manage to cope with these children,' he said and pointed at his colleague. 'We'll go and see if we can locate him, don't worry! We'll be very careful and make sure the dogs don't harm him!'

I shook my head as I watched them leave. 'Bloody hypocrites!' I muttered. 'Why did they have to come mob-handed for a fifteen-year-old boy?'

They had just left and the phone rang; it was Terry.

'Oh, Terry! Please, please give yourself up!' June pleaded. 'The police are here and they said that the dogs will savage you.'

'Huh! Rubbish!' He scorned, 'Fucking stupid things couldn't savage a flea. I hid in the hedge and they walked straight by me.'

'Please Terry, give yourself up!' She pleaded.

'I ain't going to prison!' He retorted. He said he was going to go on the run and then hung up. The Police carried on patrolling the area for quite some time but finally left empty-handed.

Several weeks passed before he was picked up by the police and charged with burglary, theft and non-payment of fines. In order to survive while on the run, he had stolen and committed several burglaries. So here we were again, back at square one! Another date was set and we went to court, again. As the number of times he came working with me had increased, he had very quickly become quite competent and capable of numerous jobs in the building trade. I told the court that he was a good worker, which was perfectly true, (when he was sober). However, this time it was prison, which of course I knew was inevitable. The judge on this occasion scrapped the fines set by the previous court, so he would have a clean slate when he came out.

A few weeks after he was sentenced, June found the situation very difficult to cope with and was sitting sobbing into her hands.

'What's wrong with you?' I asked.

Red eyed, she looked up. 'It's Terry! I just can't bear the thought of him in prison.'

'Well,' I said, 'just what do you suppose Terry will be doing right now?'

'I don't know,' she murmured.

'Shall I tell you then? He'll be sitting having a fag or cracking a joke with other inmates. In short, he'll be getting on with life and certainly not sitting bawling. So you should forget all of this nonsense!'

It gave her a very different view of things and she never had the same problem again.

During his time in prison, we went to visit him on several occasions. The strange thing was, he seemed much more settled there than when he was free. It made me wonder if he had been well and truly institutionalised. I was surprised when he successfully did several 'A' levels during his stay, although I was certain he was capable of them; he was very bright.

The Adoption.

Life goes on, so we carried on where we had left off before Terry. On a number of occasions, June had been to a fostering group and seen what she described as a lovely little boy who was being short term fostered.

'His Mother is Irish and his Father West Indian,' she said, 'so he's a nice chocolate colour and at three years old he is just right for adoption; don't you think so?' She looked expectantly at me, waiting for an answer. 'Well, do you?' She quizzed again.

'How would I know?' I said, rather exasperated. 'I've never seen him, have I?'

'Yes, but he does sound okay; doesn't he?'

I shrugged, spread my hands and sighed, 'I suppose so.'

'So shall I ask about him then?'

'Yes, if you must!' I said a rather irritated.

She made enquiries and shortly afterwards he was placed with us. 'Fostered with a view to adoption.' This was Billy; Billy John White. He was a beautiful child and looked Asian in colour and appearance. Our Pakistani neighbours were so pleased that we had taken in this little Pakistani boy. We didn't do a very good job of explaining that he was Irish/African but we didn't have to, as the summer wore on, he got darker and darker until one day she said disgustedly, 'I don't know what this boy is, but he certainly is not Pakistani,' and slammed the door before June could reply.

He hadn't been with us very long when one day he came into the house quite distressed. 'What's wrong?' June asked but he didn't answer. 'What's wrong?' she repeated.

Joe said, 'some boys have been calling him names.'

'What were they calling you?' She stormed, 'I'm not standing for that!' She opened the door, 'C'mon, show me!'

'For goodness' sake June, let it be!' I said, 'you'll just make the situation worse.'

She ignored me. 'C'mon, show me!'

They trooped out with her bustling alongside. As I followed, Joe ran ahead and pointed at two little kids about four years old: 'that's them.'

'Why were you calling Billy names?' June growled,

Looking very frightened, one pointed at the other and said, 'It wasn't me missus, it was him,'

'It wasn't me; it was him,' the other sobbed and pointed an accusing finger back.

'Yes, it was,' the first one retorted. 'You called him hot chocolate.'

'So? You called him chocolate drop.'

They returned to the house, leaving them arguing as to who said what.

She glanced at the ceiling, shook her head and said nothing.

Quite some time elapsed and on the first day I had my new van, someone ran into it. After many months and a load of wrangling, their Insurance Company finally paid up and while I was doing the repairs, I converted it into a mini-bus. I thought it would be rather nice in beige with an orange stripe from front to rear. As I was spraying the orange stripe, Billy stood nearby, watching.

'Jim!' He called above the noise of the compressor. It was normal for the children to address me as Jim. This was because June always referred to me as Jim when David was little. So, to him I was Jim and the other children just followed suit.

When David was small, we visited my Uncle Tommy who was really shocked and said, 'That's not Jim, that's your Daddy!'

David looking rather puzzled, reached and as he took my hand he said, 'Of course it's Jim, you're just silly.'

I told Tommy he was wasting his time and anyway, I didn't object at all.

However, 'Jim!' Billy called again.

I finished the stripe and turned the compressor off. 'Hello, that's me.' I said giving him all my attention.

'Do you like brown?'

I glanced quickly at the orange stripe then back at him, 'That's not brown, you Wally, that's orange!'

Blowing air in exasperation, he put his arms akimbo and looked at the sky.

'No'ah!' He said impatiently, disgusted at my stupidity and tapped his arm with his index finger, 'Brown, like on me.'

'Do you not like brown?'

He puckered his lips and shook his head. 'I only like white,' he said with a sob in his voice. I set the spray gun down and scooped him up. 'Your brown is beautiful son; I'd love you even if you were purple.' I kissed him on the cheek, it did make me feel sad because sometimes in the past when I had been bathing the children, he would tap his arm and say, 'Look Jim! I've got brown.' Then he would hold his arm against my very fair one and say, 'See?'

Being foster parents, we were fortunate in that it made us eligible for one of the Council's houses. We applied for and subsequently got, our six-bedroom, ex-children's home that was now vacant. We'd had Billy quite a while and once again set off to Somerset for the summer holidays. Unfortunately, this time it was an absolute washout. We were constantly knee deep in mud and had to resort to waterproofs and wellies.

Patsy

After the summer holidays, we were placed Patsy, a little girl of around 18 months. She was the most amazing, highly disturbed child I had ever set eyes on. She could literally climb the walls or hang onto the worktop and screech for periods of sometimes up to six hours. She had an incredible defence mechanism, especially towards men. She would blow snot from her nose but instead of it becoming detached, it would extend to around four inches and levitate so that it would wave horizontally and remain in that position for the amount of time it usually took for her targeted party to recoil in horror. She was the only child that we felt we wanted people to know that she was fostered. She had a slight deformity in her shoulders; they were very rounded and I innocently enquired if she was born like that. June told me that her mother, unable to stand her screeching, used to sit her in her cot with her back to the bars, take her left sleeve and drawing her arm across the front of her body, tie the sleeve to one of the bars behind her. Then do the same with her right arm, tying it behind her left side. It was as though she was in a straight-jacket, sleeves pulled down and tied to the bars, with her arms folded across in front of her. Her mother then either went out or sat watching telly for hours while she screamed.

During her stay with us, we had to take her for assessment to see if she could be placed back with her parents. Her Dad, her mum and her Social Worker were there. June dressed her in a little suit that she bought specially for the occasion, and we took her on the train. She looked really nice; her best ever! There was June and me, Patsy, her Parents, Patsy's Social Worker and our Support Worker, all sitting in a room with dark glass down one side. Patsy was playing quite happily and seemed really pleased to see her Mum who cuddled her briefly. A short while later, two ladies came in and explaining the procedure, said that there were other observers on the other side of the glass. Patsy's Daddy had picked her up and was standing with her by a window looking out. The room that we were in was on the third floor and outside, a building site was in progress with a crane that towered well above us. We all sat in a prearranged semi-circle of chairs and one of the ladies said to him: 'Would you like to join us?'

He didn't turn around but said to the window. 'I love my baby. If she wanted that crane out there, I would buy it for her.'

With that, he turned and came walking across the room towards us, but stopped halfway, held her up level with his face and sniffed. 'Phew!' He exclaimed and crinkling his nose, puffed as though blowing a nasty smell away, then walked over to June, held her out and said, 'Here! I think she needs changing.'

Her natural mother looked at the ceiling as though the baby had nothing to do with her, and June proceeded to change her. We all settled down and they told us to just act normally. Patsy was running around the room from one to another, accumulating the toys provided. She went to her daddy, and to my horror, he fished a large number of felt tip pens out of a box and took the tops off for her. She quickly adorned herself and her beautiful new clothes with many different colours. She ran to me with the handful of pens, I smiled sweetly and held my hand out. 'Ta ta,' I said and she gave them to me. I hid them under some papers and didn't much care how my actions were interpreted by the people behind the glass; they didn't have to take her home at the end of this episode. To my surprise, she came running back with some more which I promptly hid. She must have thought it was a good game as she brought the remainder. Despite managing to hide the pens, she was a mess, not just her clothes, she had done a fairly good job on her hands, her face and even her legs. As luck would have it, June had her usual supply of baby wipes and was able to clean her up, but not her lovely new clothes; they were a mess.

As time wore on, the natural parents, particularly the mother became quite aggressive. It seemed to me that they were digging a hole for themselves that would be impossible to climb out of. The session ended and I thought that they had destroyed any prospects of Patsy returning to them.

Our Support Worker left and as we were leaving, we said we were going to go and have some lunch. Patsy's Social worker said: 'I'll join you; I know a very nice place that quite a number of my colleagues' use; would you like to go there?' It sounded perfect so we agreed.

We were all seated nicely at the table. June had Patsy on her knee and she started screaming and wrestling with her. The more June tried to pacify her, the worse she became. I watched the waiter who had taken our order, he was studying Patsy very closely, and when he brought the vegetables, he put them on the table and stood in front of her; she was still screeching. Beaming and giving her all of his attention, he held a lolly out and said, 'Would the little girl like a lollipop?'

She slapped it so hard that it shot out of his hand and landed in a lady's soup at the next table. Both the waiter and June were so taken aback that they weren't ready for her when she swatted the plate of carrots and they went zooming across the polished floor. June was so apologetic to everyone. Her Social worker knew that she was difficult, but had never seen her in full swing. I thought that this first-hand knowledge would put her in the picture and do her a world of good. We tried to eat our dinner without much success as she got progressively worse; if that was possible! June, looking quite stressed, said, 'She can keep this up for six hours or more, we've had this at home.'

The Social Worker rifled through her bag and said, 'Oh dear, this is a no-smoking area, I'm just going down the other end to have a cigarette!' She smiled sweetly and was gone.

'Coward!' I mumbled as she went, I knew she wouldn't be returning; she never did.

It was impossible for us to finish our meal, so we had to leave as well. As we walked towards the station, June wrestled with her to no avail, making several abortive attempts to get her to walk, but each time, she flopped to the ground, squirmed around screeching and June had to pick her up again.

'I can't take her on the underground like this,' June said, still grappling with her. 'She could keep this up until we get home.'

We got a taxi and at the beginning of the hour's journey, the taxi driver advised us how to quieten her, but gave up soon afterwards. I looked at June and shaking my head I said, 'You are some woman, I could never cope with this kid - never!'

During the journey, Patsy momentarily quietened down and was quite calm. June relaxed and set her on her knee facing forward with her back to her and sighed: 'Phew! Thank goodness for that!'

Suddenly, without warning, Patsy threw herself backwards and with the back of her head, head-butted June in the mouth. Her lip swelled instantly and Patsy started screaming again. She continued screeching the rest of the way home, and for several hours afterwards.

During the days that followed, June's beautiful front teeth became really badly discoloured and finally, she had to have them out.

We had many distressing incidents with Patsy during her short stay with us. Looking through our photos, I noticed that I never ever managed to get a single one of her smiling, in fact I don't recall ever having seen her smile; how sad is that?

She was placed with an older couple for adoption but we later heard that it was very brief and broke down. I often wondered what became of her, she would be in her fifties now.

Billy had really settled in and been with us some considerable time; calling June Mummy and me Jim. As we respected all of our foster children's background, June felt that it was important that he should be told about his roots. One day, she was bathing him, and she said about him being brown. He was quite responsive and she decided this was a good time for explanations. She had a book with a picture of a black man stripped to the waist on the front. 'You know David's friend, James?' She asked.

'Yes.'

'Well, you know he is much darker than you?'

'Yes.'

'His daddy came from Africa, but your daddy came from Jamaica, that's why you are brown.' She showed him the picture. 'You see? This is what your Daddy looked like.'

He nodded knowingly. 'Um, hmm' he said, foaming the soap up in his hands.

She felt quite pleased with how she had put it over, he had comprehended very well. She dried him and was putting his pyjamas on when he asked: 'Where did you say Jim comes from?'

She smiled and patted him affectionately on the bottom. 'Go on, upstairs with you! I'll be up in a minute.'

As she approached the bedroom door, she heard him inside, saying: 'Peter, did you know Jim used to be black?'

She smiled and thought, 'perhaps it wasn't such a good idea to go into complicated explanations at this stage after all.'

We were going to adopt Billy and by law, we would have to be approved by the local Council. A lady known as the Guardian ad litem, a Social Worker, who assessed families applying to adopt a child turned up. She was a rather large black lady, very attractive, and I liked her instantly. On several occasions when I arrived home from work, she was there, getting to know how Billy functioned within the family setting. During that period, I was doing outside work and needed a bath when I arrived home in the evenings; a couple of times June said: 'Go and have a bath with your Daddy.'

I suppose it was natural for the Social Worker to assume I bathed him all the time, as that's how it appeared then. One day I came home early and she was coming out of the back room with him.

'Hello Jim,' she said, 'Look what Billy has just done for me.'

I smiled. He had drawn two figures, one of Mummy, who had waterproof coat and wellies on, and black teeth. The other was of a horrid little boy called John with jagged teeth. Identification was not a problem as they each had their names underneath. I chuckled and said: 'he's not too keen on John at the moment, he's been giving him quite a bit of trouble at school.'

She took a deep breath and drawing herself up to her full height, said: 'I'm afraid you're missing the point. He's not referring to that John. You see John is Billy's middle name and this,' she said scornfully, as she tapped the paper with the back of her hand, 'This, is Billy's negative black image.' She waited a moment, 'Can you not see what he's done?'

I looked blankly at the paper. 'No, I can't, what's it supposed to be?'

'He's taken a piece of white paper and drawn all these things with a *black* pen,' she said, 'it's his negative black image.'

'What? What a load of rubbish,' I scorned, 'What colour of pen do you want him to use, a white one?'

I thought it was a joke, but it wasn't and my remarks infuriated her. I wondered if she would, on reflection, discard the idea. I thought the drawing bore no relationship to what she suggested. Our holidays had been a washout and that was how he had seen June. The black teeth of course were the result of Patsy head-butting her, and he had said several times that John, who was a couple of years older, tormented him all the time.

June spoke to our Support Worker and told her that she was very worried about how everything was going with the Social Worker.

Our Support Worker shook her head and said reassuringly. 'You only imagine it, don't worry, everything will be fine, you'll see.'

June still kept telling me she was very concerned that no one was listening to her. I did my best to reassure her, although I had nagging doubts as well. Little incidents that took place during the visits did nothing to reassure us. Great emphasis was put on him having had a bath with me on a couple of occasions.

On the day of the adoption, we set out, all spruced up, June, Billy and me. This was a happy day for us, even though she had given us a bit of a hard time; at least the outcome would be the same. We arrived early and it wasn't long before The Guardian ad litem turned up, but simply acknowledged us with a nod and went off immediately to talk to one of her colleagues.

We talked small talk and I joked with Billy about what we will do when that big judge tells us he is adopted. I said: 'You will have to have a new birthday!'

A lady Court usher, on a mission, came bustling along, calling our name in lofty tones. 'Crowe! Crowe!'

'That's us,' I said, drawing her attention.

'The Judge wants you in his chambers!' She said urgently.

I called June who was talking to someone.

'Immediately!' The usher snapped.

'C'mon son,' I said smiling as I took Billy's hand. 'That big judge wants to see us.'

Dismissing Billy with a frantic wave of her hand, she said: 'Not the child, he doesn't want to see him, just you and your wife.'

Billy burst out crying. 'Wahhhh,' he wailed.

I was dumbfounded: 'What are we going to do with him?' I asked, looking at her then at June.

She was distressed too, and Billy continued wailing.

As luck would have it, our Support Worker arrived, and holding her hand out she smiled reassuringly. 'I'll look after Billy,' she said, taking his hand and patting it. 'You'll be alright with me, won't you?'

He stopped crying almost immediately, and the lady usher bustled to the door, and with an air of impatience, held it open with her back to it. We passed through into the judge's chambers where he was sitting behind his desk reading our file, and had other paperwork in front of him.

'Good morning,' I said as we approached.

'Morning,' he said abruptly but continued studying the page he was holding. Without even glancing at us, he gestured towards two chairs and we sat. A few moments later, he swatted the file with the back of his hand, and leaning back in his chair, with a look of disgust, he said: 'This is one of the most worrying cases I have ever had before me.'

I glanced at June; the colour had drained from her face.

He continued, 'I don't even know if yours is the best placement for this child.'

'We are the best placement for him,' June asserted.

'Misses Crowe, you can't even perform his normal bodily functions, you don't even bath the child, how could you possibly cope with him when he is a teenager, with the problem of his colour? What will you do when he reaches adolescence?'

'I,' she said, and pointed at herself, then at me. 'We, are experienced Foster Carers dealing with difficult teenagers quite often on a daily basis, and we have teenagers of our own.'

'Well,' he said, 'Quite honestly, I don't like it. I'll tell you what I am going to do. I shall make an order for another date to be set in six months' time, then we shall be able to monitor the situation.'

I said: 'If you do that, you will do irreparable damage to the child, we have told Billy that he is coming here today to be adopted -'

Cutting me short, he slammed his hand hard on the desk. 'I don't care what you have told the child; my concern is for his welfare,' he snapped.

I said, 'You could search the whole country and you would not find a more suited family; he loves us and we love him.'

He took hold of his jaw with his right hand and pondered a moment. 'Very well then,' he said, 'what I shall do is this: I shall make an order, setting a date in *three* months' time and I shall arrange for a Psychiatrist's report.'

Despite our protests, we were dismissed, that was how it was going to be. We went out into the lobby and were met by our 'Support Worker,' she smiled at June and Billy ran and took my hand.

'Everything okay?' She asked.

June broke down in floods of tears and shaking her head she said, 'No, it's not okay, it was an absolute disaster, everything went wrong, and I just knew it would.'

We walked down the stairs and as we approached the entrance doors, the guardian ad litem came up to me and said: 'Hello Jim, okay?

'No, it's not okay.' I snarled, 'Don't even speak to me.'

She went over and spoke to June, then left. When we got outside, I said: 'What did that bitch have to say for herself?'

She shook her head, 'She just said that you were very upset, and I told her that the Judge had set the date back for three months while we will have to have psychiatrist's reports.'

Billy said to her: 'You telled that judge that you didn't want me.'

I suppose that was how he saw it; he had come to be adopted and he hadn't been.

They arranged for him to go to our local clinic for assessment. Exactly what June had been dead set against from the outset, but we had to accept it. After he had been to the clinic a few times, they thought it would be beneficial if they visited us. It was early morning when unannounced, the Psychiatrist arrived at the house, and before June could stop Billy, he volunteered to 'show him round the house.'

She said she was 'Mortified,' she hadn't even got around to tidying the bedrooms up.

Billy tapped his arm and said: 'C'mon then! I'll show you where I sleep!'

He then marched up the stairs. The Psychiatrist continued standing in the hall and Billy, halfway up, turned around, put his arms akimbo and said: 'You coming then?'

June, with a gesture of exasperation, shook her head and tutted. I glanced at the ceiling then nodded towards the stairs. We all trooped up behind them and Billy burst into the first bedroom that looked as though a bomb had hit it; toys everywhere. He launched himself onto the bed and bouncing up and down said: 'This is my bed,' and pointing across the room said, 'And that's Joe's bed.'

He sprang down off the bed, scuttled across the landing into our room and was quickly hopping up and down on our bed and said: 'Mummy sleeps here and Jim sleeps there, and in the morning, I get in there, Joe gets in there and we all watch telly.'

This carried on until he had shown him around all six bedrooms. Everyone found it very amusing. The whole performance had been so normal and natural and the Psychiatrist took an instant liking to our family.

Three months passed and we were due to make our appearance at the Court again. Needless to say, we were all rather jittery. David said he wanted to come to Court as well, and in the end, the whole family went. It was the fifth of November and we lined up close to the Judge's chambers. The guardian ad litem was standing close by, we had neither seen nor spoken to her since the last Courthouse meeting. I thought that she had certainly stirred up a hornet's nest and felt quite cross with her, although I took great care not to show it. The Judge breezed down the hall and addressed us each in turn: 'Good morning, good morning,' he said, then stopped at David and asked June: 'I don't think I know this young man, is this your son?' June nodded.

'Good morning,' he said smiling, then held the door wide open, with his back to it. 'Do come in please, and have a seat.' He said.

We filed in and sat at a very long table opposite him. The guardian ad litem sat a discreet distance from us. The judge smiled as he held some papers up in one hand and tapped them.

'I've had the report.' His smile faded. 'I'm afraid we were a bit hasty last time.'

He set the report down on his desk, smiled at June, picked up his pen and said: 'You have nothing you want to add?'

'Emm, no,' she said, seemingly at a loss for words.

Peering over the top of his glasses at the guardian ad litem, he asked: 'Do you have anything further to report?'

'No, nothing,' she said shaking her head.

'Good!' He said and signed the order with a flourish.

He smiled at Billy, stood up and said: 'Your new birthday is Guy Fawkes Day, thank you very much.'

All rather dazed we stood up and there were mumbles of, 'Is that it?'

He went and held the door open again. Smiling, he nodded to each of us in turn as we filed out. 'I hope you will all be very happy,' he said to June as she passed.

When we got outside, we congratulated each other, it was a load off our shoulders.

Back again?

We were contacted by some sort of welfare worker at the prison where Terry was being held. Terry had approached him asking for therapy and said he would like us to be involved. That was a turn up; I thought perhaps all the studying had done him a world of good. We went for a couple of sessions and by all accounts there had been a big change in him. He would be a different person when he was released.

He was discharged and everyone rallied round to help him, we were so proud of his achievements. When one considered his start in life, this was extraordinary. The local Council came up trumps, setting him up in his very own flat. That quite disgusted Billy who said, 'If you hadn't adopted me, I would get a flat.' And that was very true, it was an unfortunate fact of life, foster kids got flats while our own kids floundered. However, we did everything we could by way of helping to furnish it. Friends donated numerous items, my sister gave him a very nice settee, and in a short space of time his little flat looked really homely.

He got a job as a barman, working in a rather posh Hotel, so we kitted him out with new clothes specially for the occasion, and June said he looked a million dollars. As he was now in full time employment, he asked if Sally, our friend, was still running her club.

'You know,' he said, 'where you get your bits and pieces for camping?'

'Oh, yes, she is,' June said, 'why what did you want?'

'I fancied some sort of hi-fi system, that's all.'

June said: 'I'm sure that would be alright.'

A few weeks later, we saw Sally and I said: 'Terry asked us about you, has he been to see you?'

'Yes, he has,' she said, 'he's ordered a really nice hi-fi system. Well, I say really nice, actually it was the best one in the catalogue...and the biggest speakers. I should think he's had them by now.'

I could hear little alarm bells ringing in my head. 'How much did that lot come to?'

She shrugged. 'Seven or eight hundred pounds, I think.'

I glanced skywards and thought; 'I hope he pays for it.'

The next time Terry came to visit I said: 'I hear you've got a nice new hi-fi system then.'

'Yeah!' He laughed. 'Brilliant! Four hundred watts, blow the bloody windows out!'

'Good grief!' I said, 'You'll have the neighbours complaining.'

'So? They complained and I told them to fucking shut up!'

I glanced skyward and shook my head.

'Oh, by the way,' he said, 'This is Ray,' and pointed at a friend who had arrived with him, and I nodded.

'That's my dad,' he told Ray then said, 'We gotta go in few minutes!' He turned to Ray. 'You coming up to the bar again tonight?'

Ray puckered his lips and tilted his head thoughtfully. 'Hmm, yeah! Okay.' He turned to me and said, 'Have you been up the bar where Terry works?'

'No,' I said, 'I haven't had that pleasure.'

'Cor, fucking posh gaff that; ain't it Terry?'

He didn't wait for an answer but continued, 'I was standing at the bar and said to this old geezer beside me, 'S'cuse me mate, I've got to go to the bog, 'cos I need to fucking belch!' That's how it is up there; toffee nosed load of bastards!'

'And what did he say?' I asked.

'He thought that was funny, he did, and Terry cracked up, didn't you Terry?'

Terry was laughing, a strenuous noiseless laugh. He stopped and wiped tears from his eyes and they left straight away. I didn't get a chance to tell him to get rid of Ray.

A few days later Terry came round again. 'Fucking bastards gave me the sack,' he growled.

'I wonder why?' I thought. 'What reason did they give you?'

'They said I wasn't suitable; bastards!' He thought for a few seconds, and said, 'they just didn't like me, that's all.'

'So, what are you going to do now?'

He shrugged and looked sideways. In the days that followed, we heard that he had sold the hi-fi and some of the contents of his flat.

Early on, shortly after we first had him, he got into trouble for stealing, and I had a talk with him. Sitting across a table I said: 'Terry, what exactly do you want out of life? Do you want in about sixteen years' time, someone like me to sit across a table from your child and say, 'What do you want out of life? Because mark my words, that's what will happen.' Sadly, I predicted it so well.

However, during his next visit, I thought it would be a good idea to have a chat about what was going on. 'Is everything okay with your flat?' I said and he shrugged, but didn't speak. Mentioning his hi-fi, I said, 'You do know you that can get into serious trouble for selling goods on hire purchase?'

'Pah!' He said, dismissing it with a wave of his hand. 'Fucking things were damaged! I'm not paying for damaged goods!'

He said that he was going to go to France and Join the Foreign Legion. I said: 'What about your flat then, can David have it when you leave?'

He shook his head. 'I don't know about that, there's quite a few hundred owing on the gas, then there's the electric, the Council tax, the rent and…'

He didn't have to finish, what with Sally's bits, it had to be well over a thousand pounds. A few days later, in the early hours, I heard our side gate open and Terry's voice in frustrated tones, trying to whisper, but shouting. 'Sandy! Sandy! Get in there!'

The gate closed and a few seconds later, a car sped off.

Sandy was the little terrier bitch we got for him when we thought he had settled in. Was he dumping her and going? We weren't sure, but it seemed that way; he never returned for her.

We went to see what he had arranged about the flat; it was unbelievable! Before running off, he stacked every item in the flat in the centre of the living room, and set fire to it. One of his neighbours came in and as he stood alongside of us, he said: 'It's a good job we smelt the smoke; we threw buckets of water over it and put it out; we could have all been burnt out.'

I couldn't believe the charred saturated ruin of a flat. Staring at it, I shook my head and said, 'This is unbelievable, it was handed to him on a plate, and our boys can't even get a place to live.'

June, looking really distressed didn't speak, I tugged her sleeve and said, 'Come on love, let's go home!'

The siblings.

We were placed a family of three small Southern Irish Catholic siblings, whose mother was in prison awaiting trial for drug dealing. Having Catholic children placed with us wasn't unusual, no one ever bothered to check that we were actually Northern Irish Protestants. We had six children, so of course they just assumed that we had to be Catholics; so much for their rule of placing like with like; we were leagues apart! The youngest child was a baby girl and the poor little mite had been born addicted to heroin, so June had to administer daily doses of methadone orally with a hypodermic syringe. The drugs had affected her pretty badly and she had an odd deformity. Her eyes were almost double the distance apart from that of a normal child, which made her look a bit like E.T. She was a lovely natured child, but the two older ones were very demanding. Their mother was released on bail and came quite often on visits. Anything they wanted, such as a personal hi-fi, she would bring with her on the following visit. Quite often, these were things that we couldn't afford for our kids, and that made us think she had to be still dealing.

It was just approaching Christmas and the date for her court case was growing near. She came and took the children out shopping for a day but never returned. As luck would have it, June had completed the baby's course of treatment prescribed. We were told that she had fled to Dublin with her kids. The impression we got was, 'It's not our problem anymore, is it?' We never ever saw or heard anything of them again.

Patrick.

As time went by, I found that I wasn't feeling very well in myself and following a number of visits to the Doctor's, and referrals to specialists, it was decided that a problem that I'd had in the past had now developed into a tumour, and a date was set to me to go in for surgery. Shortly before I was due to go in, we were asked to take a new born baby; three months old and was at present undergoing an operation for a hernia. The Mother had told Social Services that she would not be able to cope with him. He had a very rare disease, didn't look normal, and his life expectancy was two years. He would be lucky if he actually survived his first year.

'I have seen him already and I really don't know about this,' June said doubtfully. 'I just feel that I will be left to cope with him on my own, and it will be too much.'

'I'll help you with him,' I said. 'I can't see that a little mite like that could be such an enormous problem; what about the kids, what do they say?'

'I haven't talked it over with them yet,' she said. 'Anyway, I'm going to see him again tomorrow and Carol is coming with me; we'll see what she thinks.'

Carol was a lady who used to visit us in our old place, an old dear friend and now our next-door neighbour, but most important of all, she was a very experienced Foster Mother. They were happily chatting about this little baby and really beginning to feel quite positive.

'Patrick O'Donnel, that's his name,' June said.

Carol laughed, 'Don't tell me, he's Irish!'

June said: 'That's the reason we were asked to take him my dear, but you haven't heard the funny bit; we're Northern Irish Protestants and he's a Southern Irish Catholic; isn't that a good match?' They laughed at the absurdity of it.

'What do you think?' June asked as she looked into his cot.

Carol had frozen; she was not at all prepared for Patrick. They studied this strange looking little baby and Carol said, 'but June, you wouldn't even like him if he was normal.'

June knew that what she said was true, we'd never taken on a brand-new baby before. Patrick's rare illness was a complaint that affected the cells. His face and gums were already swollen, distorting his features. Later on, it would affect the major organs resulting in premature death. Carol really didn't know what to think. They spent some time there while he was being changed and fed. June came away more than a little depressed. When she arrived home, she told me what happened.

I said, 'Don't worry about that! I think we probably should take the little mite, God knows he needs someone, doesn't he?'

The children wanted to know what he looked like and June said, 'He's got enlarged gums, little fat cheeks, little birdie legs and toes that cross over.'

'Has he got feathers on his little birdie legs?' Billy asked.

The kids roared at this, and when the laughter died down, Billy looked round at them and shook his head, 'Well, has he?'

June smiled, 'No darling, he hasn't.'

We decided that we would give it a go and he came to us the day I went into hospital. Although I found the hospital episode quite traumatic, it was soon over and I was back home again.

We had a cot installed in our bedroom at the bottom of our bed for him, and the noise he made was amazing. 'Is he alright?' I asked, concerned at the racket.

'He's okay,' she said, 'He snuffles because of his breathing problems, but he's always done that.'

'God bless us!' I laughed, 'he sounds like the Flying Scotsman.'

I soon got used to it and as time went by, didn't even notice. The main problem was feeding him, it took hours just to give him a bottle and by the time he had finished one, it was time to start him on another. In the end, everyone did a little bit of helping with that. Surprisingly he seemed to be doing fairly well, much better than expected.

Having different people hold and feed him, seemed to agree with him, and he started to respond. We knew he would never sit up and walk or talk, or do any of the things that a normal baby would do. Sammy was now ten years old and lying on the rug in the lounge cuddling him. Waving frantically, he drew my attention as he put his mouth close to Patrick's ear and whispered, 'uh, uh, uh.'

'Uh, uh, uh,' he replied. I fetched June and 'Uh, uh, uh,' he replied again. We were delighted, we had made a breakthrough.

We were contacted very early on by a charity, and were invited to a conference that was held in a major hotel at a different venue each year. There were many children with diseases similar to Patrick's. We attended several of these conferences, they were wonderful and very informative. We had no idea that there were so many children with this type of disease.

Alice.

In the meantime, we were placed a ten-year-old sexually abused girl, put in voluntary care by her father who was unable to cope with her. She was a beautiful child, slightly oriental in appearance, this was a new thing for us, well, as far as we had been told, we had never fostered a sexually abused child before, although Tony and Sophie didn't leave much to the imagination, but they were much younger and could hopefully lose the memory of such things as they got older; this was different. During her stay, June had to take her to Hospital for therapy. Upon her return from the second visit, June said: 'It was very strange at the hospital today. I was having coffee while she was having her therapy and talks on sexualised behaviour. The Lady Therapist, red-faced and flustered, came dashing into the room calling me urgently. 'Misses Crowe! Misses Crowe!' She kept shouting. 'Yes,' I said, 'That's me.'

'Oh, thank goodness,' she gasped, 'Please come quickly and do something with Alice, she's masturbating in class in front of all the other children!' We rushed to the classroom and I told Alice to get her coat because we had to go. She had got so worked up on the talks they were having that she started this nonsense. I really don't think that stupid therapist woman has any idea what she is doing, she certainly has no control over the children.'

During all the following therapy meetings, June had to sit in, in attendance. A few months went by and we had a crisis. First of all, she defecated in the children's toy box. This didn't come to light until Joe put his hands in it and became hysterical. The second one was when she bit Patrick, leaving deep tooth marks on his forehead. The children really took umbrage at that and put a notice on her bedroom door, 'Beware! This animal bites!'

One of them went to the joke shop and bought an imitation turd and put that in her room. She created merry hell and we had to call a halt to all of that. We found it a matter of necessity to 'cover up.' In the past, the boys would wander around in boxer shorts or pyjama bottoms but under the circumstances, we considered this to be totally inappropriate, so we bought quite substantial dressing gowns for everyone, including ourselves, and especially her. She was not allowed down the stairs without her large baggy cat suit on. The event that made this necessary was: her mother sent her a pair of tiny leopard skin briefs and a baby doll top that she wore to bed. None of us had actually seen this, only June. During an evening when a number of David's friends; young men in their late teens and early twenties, congregated in the hall, waiting for him to get ready to go to a nightclub. I was in the back room and heard David bellowing, 'What the bloody hell do you think you're doing? Get back upstairs to your room!'

By the time I was on the scene, she was gone. 'What's going on?' I asked.

David said: 'That silly little bitch Alice, sneaked half way down the stairs, then jumped into the middle of us and her nightie went up round her ears, all she had on was some scanty little leopard skin briefs.'

He was furious and his friends were quite embarrassed. After a while, the children began to more or less ignore her, so the friction we'd been having between her and them petered out. A new conflict started up between her and June, and became increasingly worse, but at the same time she was ultra-nice to me. The bad times that she and June were having, were strictly reserved to when I was not present, or she would manipulate the situation so that if any conflict took place, it looked to me as though she was having a hard time, and I sympathised with her. This enraged June and we had blazing rows, not because of what she was doing, but rather that June felt I wasn't giving her the support that she so desperately needed. Of course, I, seeing only the nice side of Alice, assumed she was nice with everyone. June said I was naive and being hoodwinked, which, looking back, perhaps I was. The only other friction was between her and Joe. When the 'toy box' incident took place, he had a lot to say. Although he was about five or six inches shorter than her, he had a full-size mouth and it was a job to shut him up, so she decided she didn't like him.

We had an invitation to attend another conference but I felt that we couldn't afford it. At this point, Patrick was very low and June was manually 'sucking him out,' which meant passing a tube up his nose, down into his lungs and with a special device, sucking the fluid out of his lungs with her mouth. She had been showed how to do this during her visits to the Hospital when Patrick had his check-ups. I was so glad they had showed her and not me, just watching her made me gag. We thought there was a strong possibility that he was going to die. Our doctor, who knew our family well, said he didn't see the point of taking him into hospital just yet, as she was so alert and in control of the situation. He said that they couldn't do much more than she was doing anyway, but if it got out of her control; perhaps then. We decided to throw caution to the wind and go for it. June said, 'If we are going to lose him, we might as well have something to remember him by.'

I said, 'If you feel you can cope with him on the move, I'll help in every way I can.

She said, 'The thing is, they won't take him into Hospital because they know I'm in attendance to him twenty-four hours a day, and in fact if he did go in, the only way he would get the same personal attention would be to take me in with him.'

'He loves the van.' I said, 'He always settles and travels well and is better travelling than he is at home.'

'The van,' that we would be going in, was our large Mercedes mini-bus that had been my work van until I decided it would make a great mini-bus and converted it. So, we went and poor Patrick spluttered all the way, but still managed to smile. We were almost a day early and booked in to the Hotel anyway. It seemed that we caused something of a furore. We decided, prior to leaving, to make it the full two weeks and brought bedding with us, as we were going to 'Camp out' after the conference. It was a good job we did, because we ended up in rooms at the back of the hotel, with virtually no amenities; not at all like the other Conferences which were always five-star, but this? It was rubbish! We thought it was atrocious value for money but decided to make the most of it. We were allocated two rooms with only one double bed and no bedding whatsoever. We set our sleeping bags out and sorted the rooms as best we could. 'It's only three days,' June said.

'Let's go for a meal!' I said, 'the kids must be starving.'

On the advice of the waiter, we had 'the cheapest' substantial meal on the menu, fish and chips so the kids were quite happy with the choice. I did a bit of calculating and said to June, 'bloody hell! Do you know how much that meal cost? Sixty-eight pounds, we get a damned sight better than that in McDonald's every week, for around twelve quid.'

Her mouth dropped open and she said, 'we'll not do that again!'

The bright sunshine and the mountain air were really therapeutic. We went touring around and I spotted a McDonald's. 'Look kids!' I said,

'Anybody fancy a McDonald's?' They all cheered.

Everyone had what they usually had back home, but that was almost treble; thirty-three pounds plus. After that, we decided to buy the makings and have rolls or sandwiches.

On the second night, there was a social evening for the adults. We gave the children some money and they went off with the older ones in charge. We came in on a conversation with some of other visitors. 'Well,' a man said, 'We soon got on that phone and asked for some more blankets, and it took them ages. The television? Sometimes it works, sometimes it doesn't. One bar of soap and one towel between four of us.

'Have you got a television?' I asked, and he nodded. 'And a telephone?' I continued.

He looked at me questioningly. 'Everyone's got a television and a telephone.'

One of the ladies butted in, 'Yes everybody has, why, have you not got one?'

'No, we haven't got a television, a telephone, towels or soap, in fact we haven't even got beds or blankets, let alone extra ones! Our children are sleeping on the floor in their sleeping bags; it's a damned good job we brought all our camping gear with us.'

It turned out that we were out the back in some unused staff quarters and not even in the Hotel, but as we had already made do, we left it at that. The little group split up and we ended up sitting at the same table as a German couple in their thirties. They were really nice and spoke very good English. When we told them about Patrick, they were really sympathetic. We chatted for some time and when he said that he was worried about his dog.

'What sort of dog do you have?' June asked, always interested in the canine species.

'A German Shepherd, he's out in my car. I have to go and let him out for a run.'

'Jim will go with you, won't you Jim?' She volunteered.

Sooner than start a row, I volunteered whether I liked it or not. It actually broke the ice and we became very friendly. I said that we had an Alsatian as well, and he was delighted. They seemed to thoroughly enjoy our company.

'I will give you my address, you must come and visit, you will love it!' He said.

I was about to get another round of drinks but he insisted it was his treat. Just before he went for them, I nudged June and nodded towards the door, 'the kids are back.'

They filed through the tables towards us. 'It's our children,' she said and as they came up close, she asked Peter, 'Is everything okay darling, where are the others?'

He jerked his thumb over his shoulder, 'Just coming.'

The other couple were looking and smiling. With that Alice and Billy came up and they looked quite dark in the gloomy light. The man's smile vanished. 'Your children?' He asked, clearly perplexed.

'Yes,' June said proudly.

We sent them to the rooms where baby-sitting volunteers had been arranged in order to give the adults a free evening. Immediately they left, the lady got up and without speaking, left the table. We sat briefly in silence with her husband who, a couple of minutes earlier had been eager to buy drinks, make jokes, talk about their dog, their child's illness and said we should swap addresses. He sat staring through us as though we didn't exist. Shortly afterwards, he also got up and left. Neither of them had said a word since the kids arrived, they just left. I thought that was bizarre and whispered to June, 'If he's gone for drinks, he doesn't even know what we want.'

We were both quite puzzled by this, but after thinking it over for about five minutes I asked June, 'Do you know what that was all about?'

She shrugged and shook her head.

'Well, I'll tell you then! It's our coloured children, and I'll tell you another thing, that's the reason we are stuck out the back of the hotel in bloody staff quarters. Have you noticed the strange looks we get when we are out? It's not just that we have a massive bunch of kids; no! It's different, it's Billy and Alice!'

When we relieved the baby sitter, all the children were fast asleep. The boys were crammed into one room. We had Patrick beside us and out of necessity, we also had Alice on the floor in her sleeping bag alongside our bed. We settled down in our sleeping bags and soon drifted off as well. As we'd had several drinks that night, I woke up in the early hours to go to the loo. Dawn was breaking, casting light into our room. On my way to the loo, I did a double take. Alice was not only out of her sleeping bag on the floor, but she was absolutely naked. I quickly threw the sleeping bag over her, shook her and she looked sleepily at me. 'Cover yourself up, you Wally! Where are your pyjamas?' I whispered as loud as I dared without waking the others. I thought; 'A fine how do you do. The kids have to pass through here to go to the toilet.

We had three days with really interesting lectures, then it wound up, and upon our return, I spotted a fast-food restaurant and decided to take a chance on getting fleeced again. 'C'mon kids, let's get some grub!' I turned to June and shrugged, 'what the hell, it's only money. You can have anything you want on the menu.'

I whispered to June, 'They've been living on sandwiches and rubbish all week.' I turned back to the children, 'Puddings too, anything!'

What a pleasant surprise! We had a superb meal, far superior to anything we'd had in the hotel and it was cheaper than McDonald's. A huge portion of steak smothered in gravy, chips, salad, drinks and delicious desserts all round. It reaffirmed my opinion that the hotel was total rubbish.

Patrick's condition worsened and we had to take him to the Doctors, but once treated, his improvement was almost immediate and we motored on. By the time we got home, he was as good as he had ever been since he'd been with us.

I received a phone call from someone in Croydon. I didn't recognise the name although he spoke as though he knew us.

'Sorry, what did you say your name was?'

'It's Terry,' he whispered.

'Terry? I thought you had joined the Foreign Legion.'

There was a brief silence and he cleared his throat. 'Yeah, well, em, they chucked me out because I wouldn't follow orders.'

He said he had settled down and was really happy. He wouldn't be returning to our neck of the woods, he had a good job, a new car and was doing really well. That was good news and I felt quite pleased about that.

A few weeks later, we received a phone call from a London Police Station and June said, 'They have Terry in the police cells. There is no point in us going to visit him, he is being transferred to a local station.'

Later on, she put the phone down and smiled. 'That was the Police again, they have Terry in the cells down town and want me to take some food in for him.'

'What? They won't even feed him! That's absolutely outrageous!'

She started chuckling. 'No, it's not that, he told them he's not eating their shit, he wants his Mum to bring him some proper food!'

I laughed and said: 'Best we get down there then before he dies of starvation!'

He was released through lack of evidence. It was around this time that he changed his name to ours by deed poll and we let him come and stay with us... again!

Owing to his problem when he had alcohol, we banned him from bringing any drink into the house. If he wanted to get drunk, he would have to go elsewhere, that was the rule! It worked very well until one night we went out and upon our return, found him in the house with several of his 'mates,' all paralytic, and they had smashed all our children's bicycles playing crazy drunken, crashing games.

June shouted, 'I told you, you were not to bring alcohol into this house!'

'I didn't bring drink into this house!' He roared back.

'Well? Where did it come from then?'

His friend, ashen in colour, having just been sick in the sink, raised his head and said: 'I brought it in.'

'You had no business bringing drink into my home!' She bellowed. 'What makes you think you can do that?'

He looked at her with half closed eyes and shrugged.

'Well?' She snapped.

'We went round the shops,' his friend droned, 'Terry bought a gallon of Scrumpy cider and a bottle of whiskey, then he asked me to bring them into the house for him.'

She put her arms akimbo and glared at Terry. 'Is that a fact? I warned you! No alcohol! So that's it, get out of my house, go on! Get out!'

He started towards the door but paused and sneering down at her, said: 'Don't worry, I'm going and I won't be fucking back either!' He opened the door and nodded to his mate, 'c'mon! I know when I'm not fucking welcome!' Squinting at her he sneered and said: 'The only reason you let me stay here is because of the money.'

June looking puzzled, shook her head: 'Money? What money?'

'The money you get from Social services; that's what money!' He sneered.

'The allowance we got for you? It never looked like covering your keep because you did so much damage. That stopped when you were eighteen, we haven't had a penny for you for years.'

He didn't say anything but looked taken aback, then snorted angrily, slammed the door with all his might, and left. Well, that was that, we wouldn't be seeing him again!

Some time elapsed and we were so drawn to Patrick that in order to exclude outside interference from the like of overzealous social workers for example, we adopted him. His funny little ways were so endearing that we started calling him our Little Magic Man, and that's just what he was. His condition meant that he hadn't grown, he was still about the size of a six-month old baby and to everyone's amazement, he was now two. Not only was he still with us but in pretty good nick, considering his problems. We did have the occasional crises when he got chesty and June had to sleep with him in the living room. She found it easier to manage him when she didn't have to worry about me as well; it was important that I carried on working. As they predicted, he wasn't able to sit up, or develop in any of the ways of a normal child. We felt that he was missing so much in his little world, flat on his back all the time, even when we had him out in his buggy. Friends said we should apply for a Major buggy that could have a special seat fitted to hold him in a sitting position. We applied to the DHSS (Department of Social Services) and they said he would have to have a medical assessment. I knew that when they examined him, there would be no problem. It would be just a matter of form, so we didn't feel it was necessary for me to go as well. I was so excited when I got home from work, I wanted to know how long it would be before he would get his new wheelchair.

'I'm afraid it's not that simple.' June said.

'Why? What's wrong, did they not give him one?'

'No, they did not! The Doctor examined him and said he could see nothing wrong with him, he said he was a lovely baby.'

'Did you not tell him about his disease?'

'Of course, I did, but he said again that he was a lovely baby and had no special needs.'

'Jesus Christ!' I stormed, 'is the bloody man blind, or stupid... or both? You should have told him to bugger off, you didn't want to talk to the boy, could you see a proper Doctor now!'

'I was devastated,' she said. 'When he said he was a lovely baby for the second time, I shouted at him, 'he's not a baby, you stupid man! He's a two-year-old little boy.' I got up and put my coat on and he said: 'here, where are you going? I'm not finished yet.'

I said, 'Well I am, I'm not staying here another minute listening to this rubbish,' and I stomped out. I'm not satisfied to leave it at that, I'll see he gets his wheelchair if it's the last thing I do.'

The Allegation.

Alice was still with us and we kept getting conflicting reports from school where she had become a major problem. All the lady teachers found her impossible, but the men, including myself, found her a delightful child. She was constantly battling with June, and social services decided to enlist a psychiatrist. The conflicting reports and bizarre behaviour that were taking place, was reported to Ronald, her Social Worker. He decided that she should have regular psychotherapy at the local clinic and he made appointments for her. These were to be set in motion as soon as possible and June asked when the appointments would be, and he said: 'It has nothing to do with you, these appointments are to be with Alice; it is important that she is made to feel responsible.'

Despite our protests, that was the way it was going to be. Since we'd had her she had been taken, fetched and supervised, and this ruling meant that she would be wandering around town and we would have no knowledge of her whereabouts. We never knowingly wanted any of our children to wander around alone, so it wasn't purely because she had come as a sexually abused child. Children are vulnerable and as such, we always tried to ensure that they were either in the company of another child, or a responsible adult, and when we consider the recent findings of country wide sexual exploitation of children, didn't we get it right?

The Educational Psychologist was so worried that he asked June to approach the headmaster and ask for her to be statemented. The headmaster became very angry and said that she was a delightful child. He said he would take a special interest in her if she needed extra tuition. This was a contradiction of all the reports that had come from the lady teachers.

She was still homing in on Joe, but, even though he was very much smaller, he was certainly not lacking in volume!

I was sitting at the kitchen table writing a letter; it was a unit with bench seats. Alice came in and stood beside me, so I glanced up and said, 'Hello.'

Smiling, she said: 'Do you know what they call me at school?'

'So, what do they call you then?'

Flexing her muscles, she puffed her chest out. 'Mike Tyson!' She said proudly. (This was the time when Mike Tyson was world heavy-weight Champion.)

'Mike Tyson?' I gasped in shock. 'My goodness Alice, that doesn't sound very lady-like, it suggests that you are... well, it's not very lady-like, is it?'

As I was speaking, Joe came in the door and plonked himself down on the bench beside me. She slid onto the bench opposite and put her hands flat on the table. Joe looked at me and sticking his chin out, and giving me a cocky little smile, shook his head to and fro. He put his hands flat on the table, and started drumming his fingers lightly. I went back to my letter, and as he was drumming, Alice tapped the back of his hands lightly. He carried on drumming for a few seconds then quickly tapped the back of her hand. A few seconds later, she slapped the back of his hand. I was trying to ignore this, hoping it would fizzle out, when Joe jumped up, gave her hand a light slap and ran. She was after him like a shot, and kicked him really hard on his backside. He turned, rammed her against the worktop, and in a flash, was punching her face, she was helpless against his onslaught; all of this had taken a matter of seconds. I leapt to my feet, flung my hands in the air and yelled, 'stop!'

It stopped instantly but she was a mess, her mouth was swollen and bleeding.

'You asked for that my girl!' I snapped, 'and as for you...'

He put his hands deep in his pockets and looking at the floor swivelled from one foot to the other, 'She started it.'

I jerked my thumb over my shoulder and growled at him: 'You! Outside!' He went, and I turned to Alice and said, 'You'd better go and get cleaned up!'

After that, there was quite a role reversal, her whole attitude to Joe changed, and I was surprised to hear her asking him very sweetly if he would like to play monopoly.

'No!' He retorted.

We got regular phone calls from the Clinic. 'Where is Alice? She hasn't turned up for her appointment again.'

'How would we know?' June said. 'We didn't even know she had an appointment today. All of these dealings have been made by her social worker without consulting us, or letting us know what was taking place.'

The problems increased so we contacted her Social Worker again... and again. Apart from being utterly useless, he was totally unreliable. If we did manage to catch him, he invariably said, 'I'll seek advice on that and I'll get back to you.'

We were always left in limbo; he never did get back on any of the occasions. Several emergencies and meetings were arranged through him, but he never even turned up to any of them; not even a phone call to let us know what was happening.

Ellie was seven years older than Alice, and all the friction with her had ceased. Ellie didn't really have much to do with her anyway, as she was so far removed from her age group. The incident with Joe had certainly made Alice pull her horns in. She seemed to like my company and singled me out on quite a few occasions, and I got rather concerned about that. The only reason she never managed to get me on my own was because, invariably, Billy was with me; everyone called him my little shadow.

Owing to the fact that we always had a rule that our children were not to go out alone after dark. If there were any activities they had to go to, I, or someone took and fetched them in the car. So, whether it was boxing for the boys, or disco dancing classes for Alice with Carol's girls, there was always someone in attendance. We took her to a youth club and after the second visit, she was excluded for sexualised behaviour, so we had to concentrate on her disco dancing. Jackie brought them all back from the disco dancing class, to Carol's house. The other girls were not happy because she had been so disruptive. She hadn't practiced and had bullied the other girls, especially little Julie, the girl who was going to partner her in the 'doubles' of an impending competition. June popped into Carol's and was cross when she heard how she had treated the other girls. Our gardens were linked by a gate, meaning that home was just up the garden.

'Get home my girl, and get yourself ready, and straight to bed! I'll be up in a minute,' June said hotly.

It was a well-established fact that when June and Carol got talking, minutes can very soon turn into hours, and Alice would certainly not be the last one to notice that. She breezed into the living room where I was sitting watching television. One of the older children was nearby and I was totally unaware of the goings on at the disco dancing class.

'Hello! I'm back!' She smiled and sat across the room on the settee.

'Well, did you have a nice time?'

'Uh huh.' She murmured and smiled without taking her eyes off the TV. The program ended and advertisements came up.

I looked at the clock; 'Isn't it your bedtime?'

'Yeah, oh just let me watch the end of this advert, it's really funny.'

Almost immediately, a fresh program started.

'Oh look! Bread, brill! Can I watch it? Oh, go on! We watched it last week, don't you remember?'

She gave me a description of what happened the previous week, and I remembered all the kids watching it.

'Oh, go on! Please...? Please...?' She pleaded.

I to and fro'd my right hand considering it and thought: 'She did watch it last week; I don't suppose it will do any harm if she watches it this week again.'

'Alright then,' I nodded 'But straight to bed afterwards!'

She hopped up and down on the settee, with glee.

'Alright, alright!' I said: 'Settle down for goodness' sake!'

About five minutes into the program, June turned up.

'Why are you not in bed?' She scowled and then at me. 'Why is she not in bed?'

'Jim said I could watch Bread,' she said.

'She watched it last week,' I said defensively.

'Of course, she watched it last week, the kids were on holiday last week! I told you to get straight to bed madam, do it!' She snapped.

Alice scuttled off to bed and June looked at me, squinting her eyes, gritting her teeth and shaking her head.

'Oohh!' She scowled. 'She's been giving Carol's girls a really hard time at the disco dancing classes, the others are absolutely fed up with her, they don't say a lot to her because she's such a bully.'

I glanced at the ceiling. 'Oh God! There'll soon be nowhere she can go.'

At this time of the year, Carol's family and ours would get together and have barbecues, and it was magical. Carol's husband, Jackie and I, would get two or three barbecues going then set out a load of tables in the garden; we loved it, and so did the children. We usually started at around dinnertime and then perhaps have a swim in our above ground pool and relax in the garden right through the afternoon. Early evening, we would go indoors and perhaps watch a video, or just have coffee, it was such a nice way to wind up. Then the bombshell came, Alice accused their fourteen-year-old son of sexually assaulting her.

'What?' Jackie bellowed. 'Right! That does it, fetch the Police... right now!'

'Oh no, no!' Carol begged, panicking. 'Let's talk this over like sensible adults! If we call the Police, it could have very serious repercussions and we could suffer a great deal, especially as I don't believe one word of it... lying little bitch!'

June had taken Alice to one side and was talking to her out of earshot. Alice was looking at the ground and moving a small pebble around with her foot.

A few minutes later, June returned and said: 'I asked her exactly what happened and she now says nothing happened.'

Jackie growled, 'I bloody knew it!'

Carol said, 'I asked Simon and he said he was never on his own with her at any time, and the other children all said the same.'

'Bloody little bitch!' Jackie said glaring at her.

The incident passed, but it was the demise of our wonderful barbecues. Later on, June sat beside me and said: 'Alice has decided that she wants out of this placement, she feels she is being policed and restricted by me. I am certain she is going to make an allegation against someone else, I don't know who. I think she accused Simon but withdrew it because there were too many kids present and they could easily prove she was lying; I have a suspicion she will accuse our vicar. She feels tied down and a sexual allegation is a good way to gain freedom so that she will be able to come and go as she pleases. The best way to achieve that is to accuse someone of anything sexual; isn't that right?'

I nodded in agreement.

June phoned Ronald and they had an argument over it. The situation became so unbearable that she wrote him a quite angry letter, we talked it over, it was very much to the point and said that not just once, but on several different occasions when he made arrangements to visit, he never arrived; not even a phone call.

June removed Joe and Billy from the school. It wasn't worth taking

Sammy out as he would be moving up to a senior school in a matter of weeks. Because the letter was very emotional, we discussed it... was it too much of an ultimatum? We did actually have Alice's welfare at heart. In the end, June decided we should send it. We still feel to this day that had things been handled anyway well, we would never have had to write it in the first place. Subsequently, we soldiered on with the task in hand; the care of Alice.

Everyone that we told about the DHSS's decision on Patrick was outraged. How could they say that little Patrick had no special needs and didn't need a wheelchair? It caused such a furore and people were so disgusted; the local press ran a quite lengthy item about it and people rallied round in support.

June said 'I want to highlight that Patrick is one of the many whose needs are not being met by the Government.'

Peter had been taking guitar lessons for some time now and often played at the church along with Ellie, who had taken up the flute and singing. Our vicar, along with Ellie, Peter and several others, did their part in a charity do to raise funds for his wheelchair. Along with private donations, the amount raised was well in excess of the sum required to buy the wheelchair, so the remainder was put into a fund for children in need.

What a difference his wheelchair made; it transformed him from lying flat and unmoving in a pusher, to a cheeky, smiling little imp. Where in the past people had ignored him, they made a fuss of him, and they were able to have eye contact. Before long they were saying, 'Everyone likes Patrick.' He did get strange looks, as at first glance everyone assumed he was a tiny baby, but on closer inspection, they could see that he was in fact, a tiny little boy, a rather odd-looking little boy. June got a sticker and put it on his wheel chair. 'Why be normal' it said, and it was perfect.

In the meantime, we heard through the grapevine that Terry was living rough, sleeping among the cardboard boxes at the back of a freezer firm where he had a job filling freezers. Then he moved and was living up the tracks in a tent. During this time, he called at the house while we were out and left a large bag of personal belongings under the stairs. June looked in the bag and became very alarmed. There were large hunting knives, swords, trinkets and electrical goods. She called the police who arrived and took the bag away for examination. So, we were back to square one, taking Terry his meals down to the Police cells.

He laughed at how thick the coppers were and said: 'One of them interviewed me, trying to connect me with a number of burglaries and the theft of a very distinctive leather jacket. He questioned me for about twenty minutes or so, and when he was about to take me back to the cell, I stood up and he stopped in his tracks and said: 'Here, wait a minute! Isn't that the jacket I've just been describing?' And I burst out laughing. He didn't think that was funny, stupid bastard!'

Once again, we ended up with Terry under our roof. Probably a sort of benevolent gesture on the part of June while he was undergoing investigation for the alleged crimes, that we thought sure he was guilty of. He was discharged through lack of evidence and I had him come back working with me. However, his heavy-handed manner and chaotic behaviour became so much of a financial burden that I just couldn't carry on. There were incidents like dropping a large shifting spanner into an expensive bath that I had just installed in a brand-new bathroom. The bath and a lot of the tiling had to be replaced. He drilled into engineering bricks with a brand new, one-hundred-and-fifty-pound hammer drill, (a lot of money in those days,) when I had specifically told him to be sure to drill only the joints; it had to be dumped. The man at the repair shop said that the repairs would cost more than a new one. On another occasion, we had to demolish a doorway and I asked him to knock some of the brickwork down and take the doorframe out. This sort of thing he was damned good at, and I came around to see how he was getting on. He had virtually finished the job, all except the high bits. I looked at the doorframe, half-buried in brick rubble with long rusty nails sticking out.

'Well done!' I said, 'Best have a clear up, then get the steps and knock that last bit up the top out!'

He nodded and I left him to it, but as I turned the corner, I heard a roar from him, and before I even returned, I knew exactly what had happened. My steps were lying broken in the heap of rubble, and he was writhing around on the ground, bellowing in agony. He had lodged the steps precariously in the rubble, climbed up, they had toppled over and were broken in the process. A large nail in the doorframe, had gone right through his foot and was sticking out of the top of his trainer. Had he done what I had said, not only would we have finished the job in good time, but my steps, (perfectly good steps) would not have been broken. He would not have had a badly damaged foot, and I would not have had to take him to Hospital. The list was endless. I lost count of the number of paint pots he 'accidentally' kicked over. It got so that in the end I couldn't help wondering if he was on some sort of vendetta. Again, we stipulated that no drink was to be brought into the house and he stuck to that rule.

One night, he went off and got paralytic and when he returned, we were sure there was going to be trouble. He took our comments on his condition as a personal slur and stormed off upstairs. I thought he had gone to bed, but later, when I went to the bathroom, I discovered he had locked himself in and I was unable to rouse him or gain access; we became very alarmed and called the Police. They couldn't get any response from him either, and had to break the door down. He was a bloody mess, unconscious on the floor, his wrists slashed and there was blood everywhere. The Police called for an ambulance, and in the meantime, they wrestled him down the stairs. The activity brought him to, and he started screaming and fighting with them.

'Fuck off and leave me alone, you bastards!' He kept shouting.

June was distraught and when the ambulance arrived, she was so worried that she felt she had to go with them.

When she returned, she said, 'It's a good job I went with them. I was a bit worried because you hear stories about police beating young people up when they take them in. You would not have believed it; he was like a wild animal and ended up fighting the Police and the ambulance men. It got so bad that in the end that I grabbed his face.'

She demonstrated by clasping her own face so that her fingers were one side and thumb the other. 'Sit down and behave yourself!' I snarled into his face; 'This isn't the coppers you're dealing with, it's your mother! You know what? He sat there, meek as a lamb the rest of the journey.'

As we suspected, his cuts were not too severe. It was a token to make us feel dreadful and it certainly did the trick. We persevered with him but made a new rule; no drinking, full stop! There was a dramatic improvement in him.

David and Trevor had been away seeing a bit of the world. Even though we are not Jewish, a friend of mine arranged for David to go to a Kibbutz in Israel for a year, and Trevor went to Grover City, California. When David returned, he was looking for a place to stay and found a flat that suited extra well, but he just could not afford the rent. Terry volunteered to share with him. We had reservations, but thought if it worked, it would be good for both of them. They decided to make a go of it, and when David paid a security deposit of quite a few hundred pounds, they moved in. At first it all went well, they seemed to hit it off until, a little while later, Terry started acquiring items like a new stereo, television, video player etcetera on the hire purchase, through the new address. Then David got into trouble with the rent because Terry didn't pay his share. It got so bad that David had to call it quits. He was going to move out, but Terry's heavy-handed behaviour had destroyed a number of items of furniture, so he wouldn't be getting his quite hefty deposit back.

David invited a few friends round and, in the meantime, Terry arrived home drunk and David said, 'Terry, when I go, I am going to take the television towards some of the debt.'

Terry walked over to the quite large television and put his hand on top of it, 'What, this television?'

'Yes!'

'We'll soon fucking see about that!' He said, he picked it up and threw it to the floor with all his might. The others watched in horror but were astonished when it bounced and flew across the room. The mains lead tightened and snapped the plug out of its socket and whip-lashed as it carried on bouncing around the room. When he saw it hadn't broken, he started kicking it in a frenzy. David and his friends were so alarmed, fearing that the tube would explode, they cowered in the corner in order to avoid the flying glass. He kicked at it for some time but when it didn't break, he stopped, looked thoughtfully at the ceiling, and as though nothing had happened, said: 'I'm gonna go and make a cup of tea.'

He disappeared into the kitchen, and the others, unable to comprehend just what had taken place, got up and looked at each other. They couldn't help laughing, although, at the time, they didn't think it was funny. Despite the fact that it gave funny little splutters and the text went a bit wonky, amazingly, the television continued to work; David lost his deposit.

Disco dancing.

We were introduced to an Agency and duly approved to adopt one of their children. Annie was a little ten-year-old, and really didn't have much to endear her as she was not particularly attractive. They told us that she was sexually abused from a very early age. Initially, she came to us for respite on occasional weekends, and her visits were quite pleasant. Everything went off without a hitch. Alice was around two years older than her and they seemed to get on okay. It was close to bedtime; June was out in the garden and I was in the kitchen when Annie passed through and said she was on her way to the bathroom; Alice was following close behind.

'Emm, where are you going?' I asked Alice.

'I was just going to give Annie a hand in the bathroom,' she said.

I hooked my index finger at her, 'I don't think that's a very good idea, you can have a bath later.'

When I told June, she said, 'Just right! That's all we would need; us waiting for a child to be placed and have her sexually abused in the bath under our very noses; no thank you!'

After several visits, a date was set about three months hence for her to come permanently. Meanwhile, Alice was supposed to be rehearsing hard for this forthcoming Disco dancing competition.

June said, 'She'll have to have a new dance suit for this competition you know!'

I pondered: 'What does she wear at the moment?'

'A suit given to her by one of Carol's girls.'

'Well, what do they wear?'

'I thought you knew, they've all got new suits... and shoes. They're like a very posh swimsuit, but they cost around fifty quid and that's just for the suit!'

'Oh God! When's this competition?'

'Sunday, so we've only got three days!'

With a joint effort, we managed to get her a suit and shoes. On the

Saturday, Alice came to me and said, 'Jim, you do know that the parents have to take the children to this competition, don't you?'

'No, I didn't, as a matter of fact... damn it, I'm supposed to be working on Sunday morning. Never mind, okay, don't worry, I'll sort it out!'

On Sunday, I rushed home from work early and dashed up the stairs. I had just picked up my wash bag when Alice, dressed in her new dance gear stopped in the doorway. 'Can I have a look in your long mirror please?'

A couple of the kids were in the room across the hall so I gestured towards it and said: 'Help yourself!'

She posed a couple of times in front of it, swivelling one way then the other.

'Well, what do you think?' She asked without looking at me.

I was near the door with my back to the bed sorting some bits. I glanced, nodded and smiled, 'Looks very nice, I think you should do well.'

As she moved towards the door, she suddenly planted her hand in the middle of my chest, pushed me and laughed, 'Ah, go on!'

The backs of my knees were touching the bed and as I started to fall backwards, in an effort to regain my balance I grabbed her arm, but I was too late. As I fell backwards onto the bed, she came flying after me and my knee must have caught her thigh, giving her a dead leg. She writhed around at the bottom end of the bed, clutching her leg. 'My leg, my leg,' she howled.

I stood up, retrieved my wash bag and smiled. 'Serves you right, you silly little bitch,' I laughed and left the room.

When I came downstairs, I asked how many were coming in the car. There were three, so I thought that was all right. Any time I took Alice anywhere, I normally took someone along as a chaperone; just in case. That way I felt I had some security in the event of, an allegation perhaps?

Little Julie, one of Carol's girls, turned up at the house and June was very angry. When I came upon them, Alice was standing on the stairs, glaring at them. June spoke to Julie and pointed at Alice. 'So! She hasn't been rehearsing with you, and you feel you don't want to do a double with her?'

Julie nodded, 'Yes.'

June turned to Alice and thumped the newel post with her hand. 'Right! You think you're too big and clever to rehearse? Well, Julie doesn't want to do a double with you, she's going to do a single, so you will have to do the same!'

Alice started screaming at June. I was shocked, I had never seen her like this before. She seemed really distressed and ran up the stairs. As June walked into the kitchen I said: 'Are you sure you're not being a bit hard on her?'

She looked at the ceiling: 'Jim, I'm telling you, she's...' she searched for the words, 'She's been giving Carol's girls merry hell.'

I shook my head and said, 'I think I'd better be going now.'

I called Alice and told her to sit in the back with the other girls. On the way, I had a country and western tape on and Alice, as though nothing had happened, was her usual perky self. This was a time before seatbelts were introduced, and leaning forward onto the passenger seat she said: 'Jim, will you teach me to drive when I'm old enough?' Her tone of voice was happy.

'Yep, I reckon I could,' I replied. 'I used to be a driving instructor, I bet you didn't know that!'

She put her elbows on the front passenger seat, and jerking her head from side to side in time, she sang loudly to the music. When we arrived at the hall, the girls registered and were each allocated a number. The dancing would commence in around an hour and a half. One of the instructors, a lady, smiled and said hello. 'Are you interested in this event?'

'Ah, well, I had to bring Alice and the girls, so there you have it.'

She shook her head: 'No you didn't! Transport was laid on for all the girls; everyone knew that!'

'Little bitch!' I thought, 'she's done it again.' 'Never mind,' I said, 'I'm here now, aren't I.'

I went over to Alice and said: 'I'm going to shoot off and get something to eat, I didn't even have a chance to have breakfast.'

Looking her straight in the eye, I said: 'No nonsense! Okay?'

She nodded vigorously.

'I'll be about an hour,' I said and left.

When I returned, the dancing had started and all the girls had large numbers pinned on their backs. Alice was number 239 and the ones already on the floor were around the two-hundred mark.

'What time is this over at?' I asked her. She was leaning forward with her elbows on the chair in front, wriggling and gyrating to the music. She turned momentarily and shrugged, 'Six? Seven?'

'Do you want me to wait for you or come back?'

She sat down beside me. 'Oh no, wait, wait! I'll be on soon.'

I nodded and she got up and continued gyrating. A lot of new numbers were called out and I tapped her number with my index fingertip. 'Go on then, that's you; you're on!' I said and pointed at the stage.

'No, it isn't!' She said.

'Yes it is,' I said and tapped her number with my finger again, 'two three nine, that's you!'.

It came over the P.A. again. 'Number 239.'

'Go on then, off you go!'

'I can't, I can't!' She wailed and broke into floods of tears. She put her head in her hands and sank into a chair, blubbering. The other girls all stood gawking in disbelief. Two middle-aged ladies came over and tried to comfort her, petting her, and stroking her hair. I felt really sorry for her. Alice, the great big tough, don't give a damn, leader of the pack girl had been exposed as a phoney.

'Come here!' I said and she moved to the chair next to me.

'Don't worry!' I said, 'It's not the end of the world; there'll be a next time. All you have to do is get some practice in; okay?'

She stopped crying and wiped her eyes with the back of her hands, and as though nothing had happened, she was smiling again. 'Jim, can I go and get some sweets?' She said.

I was surprised at the change in her and said: 'ah, well, yes, em, alright then.'

I gave her some money and she went off and reappeared with the biggest bag of sweets I think I've ever seen a kid with.

I said: 'I'm going home now; do you want to stay on?'

Smiling in a distant manner, she nodded. Inwardly, I breathed a sigh of relief, I was really anxious and didn't relish the thought of the journey home alone with her in the car, I thought that could be quite risky.

'Don't go making yourself sick on that rubbish!' I said, 'I'll come back for you later; are you sure you're okay?'

She closed the bag of sweets and nodded vigorously, but didn't speak.

I returned later bringing Billy with me. The dancing was still going and I was surprised to find there were between seven and eight hundred contestants. The other girls said that they would be staying on to the end, so I collected Alice and we left straight away. I had the music playing as we motored home, but Alice sat in the back in silence. Billy was in the front with me and when we reached the town, I stopped outside the Video shop to return a rented video.

'We're parked on a double yellow line,' I told him, 'So run in and just dump this on the counter, we're not getting another video!'

That was normal procedure at the Video shop. Across the road from the video shop, there had been a major fire a day earlier, and one of the houses had been razed to the ground. As Alice was not her usual self, I was a bit concerned and glancing at her in my rear-view mirror I said: 'Are you alright back there?'

She was staring fixedly at the spot where the fire had been, and she murmured distantly: 'My friend lives next door to where the fire was.'

Billy came running and got back in the car, 'See Jim? I was quick,' he said in his cocky little manner.

When we arrived home, June was far from sympathetic. 'Well, my girl, you couldn't be bothered to rehearse, but when it came to the crunch, you lost your bottle and made a damn fool of yourself in front of everyone, didn't you?'

Alice curled her lip, and looked at the floor and but didn't say anything.

'Go on! Get to bed out of my sight!' June said, dismissing her and as she walked very slowly up the stairs, June and I went into the living room.

'Don't be too hard on her,' I said, 'She's had a pretty rough time today.'

'Pah!' June scorned, 'You and I put in a great deal of effort into getting her the dancing gear and it was way over seventy pounds, but she couldn't even put enough effort in to give her the confidence to get on the floor, so don't talk to me about rough times...we've had a pretty rough time!'

I could see no point in discussing it further, so I settled down and watched TV.

Monday was more or less uneventful, but in the evening, June said: 'What's the matter with her? She has wanted to help with everything since she came home from school. She's done the clearing up, hoovered the rooms, did the dishes, but she hasn't uttered a single word.'

'Well,' I said, 'I wouldn't worry about it! She had a pretty rough weekend and probably won't get over it in a hurry.'

The next day, she didn't say a single word, and went to her room very early that evening; first time ever. By the time she came out of her room on

Tuesday morning, it was almost time for her to leave for school, and she looked thoroughly miserable. I gave her a smile and said: 'What's wrong with you? You've lost all of your sparkle.'

She shook her head and looked as though she was about to cry, then she went over and kissed June on the cheek and whispered, 'Goodbye.'

I was preparing to leave for work, and had already loaded my van. I went out, the van was outside the drive parked by the kerb. It was a beautiful sunny morning, so I got in and wound the window down. A matter of seconds later, Alice was passing by, and she strolled across the pavement, and leaning in the window, she kissed me on the cheek.

'Goodbye,' she whispered, almost inaudibly.

I touched my cheek where she had kissed me, and I watched her walking slowly down the road.

'That's strange,' I murmured, 'she's never done that before.'

I set off to work at Margaret's house and never thought any more about it. About mid-morning the phone rang and Margaret, looking very concerned, came to fetch me. She put her hand on my forearm and said, 'it's June; Alice has made an allegation against you.'

'What? Against me? Ah, Christ! No!'

As I said it, I felt the blood drain from my face and went into a daze. I picked the phone up; June was sobbing.

'She told them that you said you wanted to screw her, she said you pressed her down on the bed and said you wanted to screw her, please tell me it isn't true,' she pleaded.

I felt like crying. 'It is absolutely not true,' I said.

My first instinct was to scream, 'What a load of crap!' I thought for a moment then said: 'What's the point in saying it's not true, is anyone going to believe me? They always say you have to believe the child.'

'You'll have to come home! Social workers are coming to the house this afternoon, they have to do an investigation.' I nodded; she was still sobbing.

'Jim? Jim?' She called as though she thought I was gone.

'Yes, I'll come home straight away; when did she say all this?'

'Yesterday,' she said softly, 'Monday morning.'

'So, that's why she acted so strange last night and this morning.'

'Just come home!' She pleaded.

'I'll see you shortly, I'll come home straight away.'

I had just been to the delicatessen and got one of their scrumptious rolls; Turkey, salad and coleslaw; the works, as I had told the girl making it. I just couldn't face it now, the half I'd ate prior to the phone call felt in jeopardy, I was quite queasy. Margaret was really sympathetic and understanding. I told her what was taking place, gathered my gear and left. When I arrived home, Emma, our Social Worker was already there.

'Hello,' she smiled a sympathetic smile, I shook my head and glanced at the ceiling; she knew the trouble we'd had with Alice.

She said: 'I'm on your side, it all sounds too ridiculous for words.'

June told me she had phoned Margaret and asked her to come to the meeting as well. I appreciated that, because I knew she was a very shrewd lady; she was observant, and I wasn't thinking very straight at this juncture. While we waited, June brought in tea and biscuits and we chatted.

Emma said, 'I remember a young girl called Chelsey, she was virtually the same as Alice, she even looked like her, and she made an allegation too. I wonder what became of her?'

Ronald and his team leader arrived, unlike in the past when there was a crisis, and he never bothered to materialise, he actually turned up! Then of course, with a mere hint of 'sexual abuse,' he would, wouldn't he? I was not the slightest bit nervous; my conscience was clear; I had done nothing wrong.

As we drank our tea, Emma, making conversation said to Ronald, 'We were just talking and I remembered Chelsey. She was very similar to Alice, wasn't she? I was wondering how she was doing; do you ever hear anything of her?'

'Oh, I don't know!' He said abruptly, 'she's probably lying in a gutter somewhere, for all I care.'

I looked at him with disgust, and shaking my head I wondered just what the hell a despicable good for nothing of his sort was doing in child care, masquerading as a social worker.

'So, what is this allegation about?' I asked.

He said, 'On Monday morning, Alice told her teacher that you said, 'I have a loving wife and loving children and a twelve-year-old foster daughter I want to screw.'

'Is that right?' I said, 'well, can I just say, that is not the sort of thing I would say! There are a lot of ways I would describe June, but that certainly isn't one of them.'

June gave a nervous laugh: 'That's a fact!'

I thought for a second, 'Screw? That word isn't even in my vocabulary; it's a child's word, isn't it? I don't think I have ever used it in that context.'

'I've never heard him use that word...ever,' June said.

'It is a sort of a childish expression,' Emma concluded.

'Where was this conversation supposed to have taken place; in the bedroom?'

Ronald moved forward in his chair. 'No! She said there was an incident in the bedroom when she felt uneasy. She did say that you have never actually touched her. No! This conversation is said to have taken place in your car.'

'That's not possible! I have never been alone in my car with her, and correct, I have never ever touched her!'

'She said it was when you were bringing her home from the Disco competition.'

'What? No, Billy was in the car with us when I brought her home.'

'But weren't you in the car alone with her when Billy returned a video?'

'Uh, yes, very briefly.'

'And did you have a conversation with Alice then?'

'Eh? Yes, I did!'

'Can you recall what that conversation consisted of?'

I thought for a second but before I could reply, June prompted me, 'Just small talk?'

I nodded and looked at her; she was under real stress. 'She's afraid I'm going to incriminate myself,' I thought, 'What chance have I got if even she doubts me?'

'Where is she now?' I asked.

'She has been taken to a place of safety.'

'A place of safety?' I echoed.

'St. Catherine's; it's a rather nice children's home, with caring staff who will look after her very well,' he said.

'I've heard about these 'Places of Safety,' some of the stories would make your hair stand on end.' I said sarcastically.

June was shaking her head vigorously, mutely telling me to 'Shut up!'

'If all these things happened on Sunday, how come she was home with us on Monday night? Surely you must have considered her to be in moral danger.' I said.

He cleared his throat. 'I wasn't notified until this morning.'

'And why were we told nothing of all this?' I said scornfully. 'When are we going to see Alice? I want to see her, face to face!'

Looking doubtful he said: 'It would not do any good at all if you confront her or start calling her a liar and things like that.'

'And why shouldn't I,' I thought and then I said, 'Well, I think it's important, both for her welfare and mine, that a meeting be arranged as soon as possible.'

'What good do you think a meeting would do?' He asked. 'What do you think would happen?'

'I think she would probably throw her arms around us, start howling, say she was sorry and then we could all go home.'

'I don't think it would work out quite like that,' he said doubtfully.

June said, 'Jim always got on very well with Alice, he loves her dearly and he is very worried about her and what's to become of her.'

The team leader spoke for the first time. 'We understand that and we shall arrange a meeting just as soon as it is humanly possible.'

Did they believe me? I had my doubts, but they did seem quite sympathetic, and she had already changed her story from the bedroom to the car, which was a very strong point in my favour. They gave the impression that this was merely a hiccup in our fostering. I didn't feel angry with her, I thought that she had gone to school, told a load of lies, regretted it and now she was unable to do anything about it; I was worried about her in this, 'Place of safety.'

Emma hadn't had much to say during the meeting. I think Ronald's remark regarding Chelsey had shocked her into silence, but even so, I was glad of her moral support. There wasn't much more to be discussed. Alice had said that I had said things, which I denied, and they had done their inquisition and got up to leave.

Margaret became very insistent. 'Get a time from them! They're going to leave and you will hear nothing; make them set a time!'

I followed them to the door. 'When do you think you will get back to me?' I asked.

'Don't worry!' The team leader said, 'There will be no secrets! We shall be back in touch within forty-eight hours.' They waved and left.

When we returned to the living room, Margaret said, 'They were going to leave without giving you a time when they would get back to you.'

'Well,' June said, 'At least they are going to get back to us within two days, so that's not too bad. Do you know what the strange thing is in all of this? The one that she will miss most is me.'

'St. Catherine's, a place of safety?' I said shaking my head. 'It'll be a place like the one Terry was in when he lived in the loft for six weeks. Wait a minute, St. Catherine's? Is that not the place that we went to visit Norman Mooney and he pulled you out of a chair you were going to sit in and said, 'Don't sit in that chair, that's where they all have it off!' Remember? You came out of it as though it was on fire.'

She was shaking her head, 'No, that was a different place but you can bet your boots

it will be something similar.'

Forty-eight hours came and went and we heard nothing except that Alice was being ferried by taxi, twenty miles to the school she had been at while she was with us. She took great delight in mentally torturing Sammy by telling the entire school that I had sexually abused her so that he felt like a figure of fun. Joe and Billy had been spared this agony; June had removed them because of the previous trouble. The days went slowly by and still nothing. I should say that they were the most traumatic days of my life, even the cancer paled to insignificance against this, and June was having a hard time too; she just didn't know whether it was true or not. She came to me one day and held my head with her hands. I can only assume that she felt that if our eyes stayed in contact, I wouldn't be able to tell her a barefaced lie.

'I have to know if it's true! Did you say those things?'

She looked into my eyes for a long time, and said: 'I have to listen to her side of it too.'

I said: 'I do understand what you are going through, but believe me, all I can say is that it's not true and you have to take my word for it...' I didn't get a chance to finish, she clasped my head to her bosom and said, 'I believe you.'

Each time I went out she quizzed me, 'Where are you going? What are you going to do?' I think she feared that I was going to commit suicide, and

I have to admit, I felt that life was just not worth living; I had never felt so low.

We had bagged up all of Alice's belongings, and they were cluttering up the dining room.

'Shall we take Alice's clothes and stuff to this...St. Catherine's?' June said as though thinking aloud.

'Hmm, yeah, that's a bloody good idea,' I agreed.

As this was a spur of the moment thing, it was after 7.30. PM. And as it was quite a jaunt, we thought that by the time we would get there, Alice would more than likely be in bed, but it didn't matter if we didn't actually see her; in fact, it would probably be better if we didn't. When we arrived, a young girl with a half-smoked cigarette in her mouth opened the door. My first impression was that this place was not keeping a tight control; 'a young girl like her smoking, and indoors?'

She stopped long enough to take the fag out of her mouth, but carried on chewing her gum. 'Yeah?' She quizzed,

'Oh God,' I thought. 'We don't permit smoking, or chewing gum.'

June said, 'We've brought Alice's clothes!'

She swung the door wide and without speaking, jerked her head towards the inside and we followed her in. There was a group of young people sitting around a table, all smoking, and one of the young men had his feet up on the table. I glanced at the ceiling in disgust and thought: 'Is this how they are supervised, all sitting around smoking with apparently no one in charge, and at this time of night?' The thing that worried me was; this lot had to be all slightly older than Alice. To my amazement, the girl that had shown us in, introduced us; this was the staff! 'God,' I thought, 'This bloody lot needs baby sitters!'

'Alice?' One of them said, 'Oh, no! She's not in yet! She won't be in until half ten, eleven; she was picked up at about...'

'About half seven,' another one interrupted.

'Picked up?' I said, rather puzzled, shaking my head.

'Yeah! Her boyfriend picks her up in his car.'

'Boyfriend? Car? How old is this boyfriend for goodness' sake?' I quizzed.

One of them shrugged, 'Twenty I suppose.'

'Bloody hell!' I exclaimed, 'Hasn't any one thought that this is out of order? She's only twelve years old! Where do they go in this car?'

The two who had spoken, perplexed at my attitude, looked blankly at one another as though it was perfectly normal for a twelve-year old girl to go off in a car with a twenty-year-old. The whole thing shook me rigid. I could not comprehend what sort of lunatics had dreamt up this 'Place of safety?'

Later in the week, June received a phone call from the 'place of safety,' and they assured her that Alice was perfectly fine. They said that the time she had spent with us had really been a boon to her, and it showed so much in her general behaviour.

June put the phone down and said: 'That was the social worker from Alice's place of safety. I told her I was worried about her going off in a car with some young man that nobody seems to know, and guess what she said?'

I looked blankly at her, shook my head and shrugged.

Screwing her mouth up in disapproval she said, 'Well I'll tell you what she said: "Oh, don't worry about that Misses Crowe! Alice will be perfectly fine, we have seen to it that she has an adequate supply of condoms, so there really is no problem." I ask you; this kid can't even use a sanitary towel properly, apart from the fact that she's twelve years old!'

I was disgusted and said, 'The thing that makes me sick, is the fact that if we did something like this with a kid, we would be publicly slaughtered by the Social Services and the Media, and rightly so!'

'Absolutely!' June said.

A few days later, the Police banged us up in the middle of the night. 'Is Alice here?'

That was a surprise. 'No,' June said, 'she hasn't been with us for several weeks.'

'Sorry to disturb you Ma'am,' the Policeman said, 'But she's gone missing you see, so we have to check on her last known address.'

She didn't turn up for school the next day, and was missing for the best part of a week.

'Bloody place of safety my ass!' I scowled.

At the end of five days, she was picked up by the Police, drunk in a public house at around eleven thirty at night. She became hysterical and was throwing jugs of water over the customers. The information we received via the grapevine was: they were considering a secure unit for her and that enraged me.

I said: 'These idiots have created this situation by letting her run amok and now they're talking about locking her up.'

A few weeks later, we were awakened in the middle of the night again. I came half way down the stairs in time to see Ellie closing the front door.

She looked ashen. 'I just hope that bloody little cow pays for this!' She said venomously.

'What's wrong? What is it?' I asked.

June said, 'It's Alice; she's gone missing again!'

I said: 'She'll end up pregnant, or she'll get Aids, that's what'll happen.'

This time she was missing for two days. Our social worker kept us posted about any events that were taking place, although we seemed to be getting the news before anyone else, via the police. Weeks passed and we heard nothing from the team leader or Ronald.

Our Social worker said she was doing everything in her power. Our numerous friends in social services were doing all they could. Alice had changed her story several times and now no one believed her.

'Do you know what?' I said to June. 'When a Social Worker says she has done everything in her power and she has done nothing, she ceases to be a Social Worker. What's the point of having her? She's no good to you, is she?'

'It's not up to her, she really can't do anything,' June said sympathetically.

'It seems to me that they have all washed their hands of this,' I said, 'and Alice is being destroyed in the process.'

As time went by, Patrick, with his funny little ways, was getting more and more of a character. He was quite mobile, in the sense that he could scuttle across the floor on his back. We gave him the run of the lounge and at meal times when we sat in the dining room, he would shuffle to the door and holler, 'Eh! Eh!'

June decided it was time for him to have his place at the table and set him up in his wheel chair and liquidised a small dinner for him, that made him and us very happy.

One day, we were out in the van and I had an Irish tape playing. June, as usual, was nursing him and he was happily kicking his feet in surprisingly good time to the music. It was an auto eject player, so when it came to the end of the tape, the radio automatically came on and Jimmy Young was reading out one of his recipes. Patrick seemed restless and June caressed his hair, 'are you all right darling?' She cooed.

'Gurr,' he growled and tried to pull his head away.

'Oh!' She said, surprised. 'What's wrong?' She stroked his hair again, and he did the same again.

'What the devil's got into him?' I chuckled.

She said, 'do you know what? I think he wants the music back on,'

I turned the tape over, it started playing again and he immediately resumed kicking his feet in time. She looked at me and gave a silent little chuckle and stroked his hair; he carried on happily kicking his feet.

'Funny little so and so,' she smiled.

'Well, who'd have believed it?' I laughed.

Trevor didn't come very often these days because he was living quite some distance away and because of that, he really hadn't had very much to do with Patrick and didn't know him very well; as usual Patrick was on the rug.

Trevor said, 'Peter, you've got to hear this record, it's brilliant!'

It had been playing for a while when June said: 'That record is rubbish!'

'What are you talking about?' Trevor said, 'that's a damned good record, isn't it Peter?'

Peter didn't get time to answer.

June said, 'It is rubbish! Even Patrick doesn't like it.'

Trevor spluttered and looked at the ceiling in disbelief. 'And just how would we know Patrick liked it?' He said.

I had just entered the room and she said, 'Jim, put Patrick's record on!'

Trevor was smiling and shaking his head. With the first chords of: 'Put your money where your mouth is,' by Sailor, Patrick flexed his little arms and began kicking his feet up and down in time. I cranked it up and he started banging his arms on the floor, first his arms then his feet. He did it so vigorously that he was doing little flips across the room. Everyone roared with laughter and that seemed to give him fresh inspiration. He began shaking his head from side to side as well. The record ended all too soon and even Trevor had to concede defeat. He picked Patrick up and threw him up and down.

'Oh, you are a little devil!' He laughed and Patrick laughed with him.

Patrick's natural mother Molly, kept in touch, and on odd occasions, came to visit and each time, she said: 'Patrick will have a much fuller, longer life with you than he ever would have had with me.'

She was really keen to raise funds for the society that had taken such a keen interest in him, and arranged a dance at an Irish Club. Obviously, we would be going and we talked Carol and Jackie into going with us.

June said, 'we might as well make an evening of it, let's go for a nice meal and then go on to the dance!'

Jackie picked us up in his car and we motored into London. We had a problem finding a parking space and ended up in the N.C.P. carpark at Westminster, under the Houses of Parliament, then caught a cab to a Steakhouse and had a nice meal. From there we went by taxi to the Club. The dance was a bit reminiscent of the dances back home in Ireland, but it wasn't really Carol and Jackie's cup of tea. The crowd became more and more inebriated as the evening wore on. One of the ladies spoke to me and when I replied, she spotted my accent.

'You're not local are you, where do you come from?' She enquired in a broad Irish accent.

'County Down, Northern Ireland.' I replied.

'Och, you poor thing!' She said sympathetically. 'And sure, it doesn't matter if you're from up there, we're both human, aren't we?'

I smiled and said, 'Well, that's true.'

Her husband interrupted. 'Aye, as long as you're not English, oi hate de fuckin' English.'

I smiled and shot a sideways glance at Jackie. Jackie didn't understand the man's accent, and asked: 'What was that?'

I said: 'Oh, he just said he knew I wasn't English,' and Jackie nodded in agreement.

To our surprise, the dance raised over seven hundred pounds and June received the cheque. The dance was still going when we left.

The next day we heard that after we left, all hell broke loose and the Police were called. Nearly everyone spent the night in the cells. Carol and Jackie would not have been amused had we joined them. Still with all, we thought Molly had done a marvellous job. We warmed to Molly and she came more often to visit and see Patrick. Several times when cuddling him she said, 'Sure she looks after you better than your mammy ever could.'

Molly along with us, took part in the making of a video which was used by different authorities as a teaching video. While we were doing our lectures, people often commented that they recognised us from the video; that was quite nice.

Due to the rapport, we built up with Molly, she asked June if she would accompany her to court, she had to go because of her two little girls; Patrick's older sisters. They had been removed and adopted by a Jewish lady who June had met some years earlier. Two little Irish Colleens raised by a Jewish lady? The mind boggles! I thought that was a bizarre choice as increasingly, with all the 'Political Correctness' that had mushroomed, especially within the borough that we fostered for, it was unbelievable! We were discussing the upcoming court case and Molly asked about the lady who had adopted her girls: 'What is she like?'

'She's a big lady and she looks Jewish.' June replied.

Molly got more and more worried about attending court and June said, 'Don't worry, I'll go with you, I'll just take my knitting along.'

So, it was agreed. On their way into the courtroom, as June and Molly walked through, the big lady was sitting in the top row of chairs at one side and June, recognising her, immediately thought she had positioned herself in order to have a look at Molly who she had never seen. Molly spotted her and said, 'That's her! Isn't it?'

June, instantly on her guard, said, 'What makes you say that?'

'You said she was fat.'

June never offered any further information and they proceeded on into the courtroom.

While the court was in progress, Molly and June had to wait in a side room, and Molly was permitted to listen to the proceedings on headphones.

'Oh! The lying old bitch!' She suddenly gasped. 'That was her; she's told the judge that you identified her to me.'

June stopped knitting and looked blankly at Molly. Molly was gripping her headphones. 'Oh! Oh! Oh!' She gasped, 'They're coming to get you.'

June was shocked and put her knitting away. Shortly afterwards, they came and ordered June to go with them. When she entered the courtroom, she was told to take the witness stand and the Judge informed her that it was very wrong of her to have identified this lady to Molly, and he told her that she would have to sign a statement, swearing that she would never again divulge to anyone, any knowledge of her whereabouts and if she did, it would be a criminal offence!

June was adamant and said that she had not identified her, and she refused to sign any documents to the effect that said she had. The judge became quite angry and as he dismissed her, he said she would have to return the following week and he would deal with her then.

The following week was extremely distressing for her, and me. To say I was furious was an understatement. I wrote the following letter to take with her:

Judge ----- *February 14th*
Dear Sir,

Have you ever been accused of lying? I'm sure you have not! It is an extremely harrowing thing, especially when you are an innocent party. This was graphically borne out during a week of sleepless nights following the accusation against my wife in court last Friday. She has been, in a sense, accused and sentenced for something she did not do; on an assumption!

Mrs B. as I have come to know her, assumed that my wife identified her to Molly, who my wife went to support. I know from some fifteen years' experience in childcare that my wife would not, either knowingly, or unknowingly do such a thing.

My wife, who sits on Adoption Panels, is very aware and alert when it comes to situations of this kind. I have never met Mrs B. but I knew quite a long time ago that she was Jewish; my wife met her in 1986. We were aware then that it would be indiscreet to divulge any information to Molly. Molly did not know that she was Jewish until several years later when she was informed by social services. The reality of the situation is that Mrs B. looks and is recognisable as a Jewish lady; even to Molly. Molly neither needed nor got any prompting from my wife. Having known Molly for the past six years, I am certain that, had my wife been stupid enough to identify this lady, Molly could have found that very distressing and that would not be in anyone's interest.

The unfounded accusation made against my wife, has caused her and our family untold misery. She feels that everything she has worked for is being demolished. She was informed that she was lying and then told to sign a document to verify it. How can she have the respect that she has to have in order to carry on with her very valuable work on the adoption panels if she is branded a liar? I fail to see how she can sign anything whilst her character and good name are in question. Neither she, nor I, see anything wrong in the document; it is the circumstances surrounding it that makes her unable to sign it.

This all comes at a time when I am supposed to be convalescing after a serious operation and finances could be better. She sought legal advice and was informed that Legal Aid would not be available as she was not a party to the case. We find that she now has to go unrepresented or face the possibility of unknown legal fees, which at this moment are out of the question. My wife did not attend Court as a friend or to collude with Molly, but specifically at Molly's request. We have over the six years that we have known Molly, supported her in any way that we could and always encouraged her to see Patrick, her very disabled son, whom we adopted. This relationship resulted in us making a teaching video which Molly took part in. We have made other teaching videos that are used nationally, so it is not a case of June being silly or indiscriminate, rather that the assumption of her being so, was wrong!

Yours etc.

June went the following week, armed with my letter and I said it would be a good idea if the judge asked her if she has anything to say, to read it aloud. Upon entering the court, before she could even approach the bench the Judge said, 'Stay right there!'

She didn't get a chance to hand it to him, she was dismissed and told to leave the court room.

Sandra, a quite high-ranking Social Worker and a very close friend, had accompanied her. After June was dismissed, they went for coffee and she showed Sandra the letter. When she read it, she bit her lip and smiled. 'It's the closest thing to a love letter that I've ever seen.'

Even though June still felt quite tense, she laughed.

We had a meeting regarding Annie and they told us that at the moment, they would not be able to proceed with our adoption owing to the seriousness of the allegation that Alice had made against me. It would have to be put on hold until that was cleared up. I understood and fully agreed with their decision; I would have done exactly the same. During the meeting, they were so shocked at how we were being treated that they said they would arrange a therapist to see us; me in particular, as I was really feeling the stress, and we thought it would be a good idea if Emma came to these sessions.

The Therapist, a lady in her thirties who did freelance work, as well as working for an authority in the Midlands, was shocked when we told her how we had coped with Alice and did not see eye to eye on how our authority had handled (or should I say, mishandled) everything. I was surprised to find that these sessions helped. It was the little subtleties that she pointed out; things that pinpointed Alice's strange behaviour and the fact that she had very often tried unsuccessfully to single me out.

We were more or less, arranged in a little group, and the Therapist said: 'If I decided to make a play for Jim,' she pointed at Emma, 'You would know,' then she pointed at June, 'You would know, in fact everyone would know, except Jim, that's how it is.'

Several times she remarked how dismayed she was at the way we had been treated by these social workers and said: 'We have a rule where I come from, when an allegation is made, it is investigated. They have a meeting within twenty-four hours with all parties present. None of this rubbish where a child is secreted away. Then if it is true, it usually comes out with the confrontation and if it is false, that also comes out at such a meeting. We find that this is the best way to deal with these things.'

A period of six weeks elapsed and finally, we were got in touch with regarding Alice. A meeting was to be arranged at the Hospital where she had been having therapy with a lady psychiatrist. Emma came to the house to arrange this and Ronald, her social worker was also invited (and wonder of wonders; he actually turned up!) We sat in silence for a short time while June made tea. Then I asked him how Alice was at the moment. I was amazed when he said that he didn't even know about her absences. I thought that was extraordinary when we consider he was supposedly her social worker and responsible for her welfare!

'Now let me get this straight,' I said. 'You haven't seen Alice since when?'

'Since the meeting here, the day after she made the allegation.'

'What?' I spluttered in disbelief. 'Are you telling me that you picked her

up and took her to this place of safety and haven't set eyes on her in the past couple of months?

'Yes.'

'What are you doing here supposedly looking after her welfare?' I said, 'you know damn all about her, or this case. What will you say? 'I know all about it, I read it in the News of the World.' I find that absolutely disgusting! No wonder she ran off and acted how she did, she must have been tearing her hair out, wondering what was happening.'

He didn't reply and the others didn't say anything either, I assume they thought I had said it all. I was amazed that he hadn't seen her, but I have to say that when I thought it through, I was not surprised. I thought that this conjured up a very accurate picture of this unprofessional, uncaring, useless excuse for a Social Worker!

We attended the Hospital at the time designated and sat in the waiting room. Finally, Ronald turned up...alone!

'Where's Alice?' I asked.

'Ah, hmm!' He cleared his throat. 'She couldn't come, she wouldn't get in the car.'

'Then what the bloody hell are we doing here?' I growled.

June squeezed my hand. 'No, don't,' she whispered and shook her head, so we sat in silence and he left shortly afterwards. A little while later a psychiatrist lady was ready to see us, would we go in? We wondered what would come next. There were just the three of us in the room but having had previous experience of meetings like this, I had no doubt that furtive eyes were watching from behind the glass panels. She leaned back in her chair and taking on an air of authority, she said: 'Alice feels that she is not yet ready for a meeting, and I am inclined to agree with her.'

I raised my eyebrows and said: 'And when, if ever, do you suppose she will be ready?'

June said, 'Her social worker said she wouldn't get in the car, just who is in charge? You don't ask a twelve-year-old girl to get in the car, you tell her!'

The psychiatrist lady was very understanding and said, 'Alice is a very confused girl, sometimes she thinks you said things, and other times she can't remember if you said anything. She said that you were always nice to her and she doesn't want to hurt you.'

'She has a very strange way of showing it,' I said.

'We shall arrange another meeting because I'm certain she does want to see you,' she replied.

So that was it, we arranged to have another meeting, and as soon as we left, June said, 'do you know who that was?'

I shrugged and shook my head, 'No, should I?'

'Well, she's that stupid woman who ran into the room calling for me when I was having coffee. 'Misses Crowe! Misses Crowe! Please come quickly and do something with Alice. She's masturbating in class in front of all the other children.'

I glanced at the sky, and laughing I said: 'Ah well, we're in good hands then, ha, ha, ha.'

Several weeks went by and we heard nothing, then another meeting was set up to take place at the Hospital. We went again and were shown into the same room with the psychiatrist lady; Ronald joined us shortly afterwards.

'No Alice?' I asked.

'Well,' the psychiatrist said, 'Alice still feels that she is unable to take a confrontation at this moment in time.'

'And just when will her moment in time be?' I asked sarcastically.

'She is still a very confused girl; I'm inclined to believe that this incident was all in her mind.'

When she said it, Ronald nodded in agreement.

'Well, I don't think it, I know it!' I said, 'So when do you think a meeting can take place?'

'I have no doubt that we can arrange a meeting in the future,' she said reassuringly.

'Do you know what I think?' I said and looked around them all, and they shook their heads.

'I think that you lot are pussy footing around this girl, she is not being made to face up to anything that she has done, and this is certainly not preparing her for life when she has to make a go of things on her own. It's a bit like a war, with Alice leading the charge, and you bunch of idiots behind her, egging her on, and off she goes galloping straight to hell, because mark my words, that's exactly where she's headed! I'll tell you this though, hell will freeze over before I set foot in this dump again!'

June was flabbergasted. I got up and extended my hand to her; she reluctantly took it and we left as soon as I had said my piece. I knew Ronald hadn't got a clue about what was going on, and he had made it very clear that he didn't give a damn either. Her welfare, just like ours and Chelsey's, was of no interest to him.

There was a meeting called with a Police presence and all the Social Workers involved in the case. During the meeting it was decided that there was no case to answer; astonishingly, we were not invited!

We were informed, 'you will receive a letter to that effect in due course.'

'I don't need a letter to that effect,' I said to June, 'I feel completely vindicated in this matter, I did nothing wrong!'

'Oh, yes we do want a letter!' June said. 'Suppose we want to foster for another Borough, or adopt a child, or anything for that matter, a letter like this clears it all up.'

'Well, when you put it like that, yes, I suppose you're right,' I conceded.

Little did we realise then that it would be over three years before any such letter would materialise, and we would never see Alice again. She never did 'face the music,' for what she did.

Annie.

With that episode gone from our lives, but certainly not forgotten, we had to put it behind us and concentrate on the new task in hand...Annie. We found that the past events, which, when they happened to other families, it tore them asunder and finished them as foster families. It had the reverse effect on us, we felt stronger and more able to deal with any situation that presented itself. We had come through the very worst scenario and survived! Because of that, we were asked by several different authorities, to give lectures 'on allegations,' which we did.

Annie finally came. She was a little odd bod of a person but seemed quite nice though. Being sexually abused, we knew what we were up against; or did we? She had been to a special centre for disturbed children for some considerable time and was now being taxied on a daily basis, along with other pupils, to and from a boy's school; she was the only girl.

'The only girl?' I thought, 'that's very strange.' Especially when I considered it from a policing angle, but then we had to accept that these 'experts and specialists' know what they are doing. Still, I had nagging doubts. In the early stages, she fitted in very well, although I felt that she was a bit like a zombie. Whatever you told her to do, she did it without hesitation. I thought that was perhaps the way I saw her until June said that she was like a non-person.

'She's like a ...'

'A zombie,' I prompted.

'Yes! She is, isn't she?'

She hadn't been with us very long, when she was moved up to a new 'normal,' mixed school. So, after the summer break, she would be going to Alice's old school.

Ah, summer! We set off again to Somerset as we normally did, to the same site as our fostering friends. In the early stages of the holiday, I noticed that people were giving me strange looks. I smiled at one lady and said, 'Good morning.'

She threw her head in the air and turned her back on me. On the third day, I was sitting in the awning reading the Daily Mail when June came storming in dragging Annie by the arm.

'I have just been talking to Connie,' she scowled.

Connie was the foster Mum who had actually set the campsite up for carers.

'And this...this thing,' June hissed, gesturing at her. 'She has been going around the campsite telling everyone that you sexually abused your previous twelve-year-old foster daughter and that Sammy, (our fourteen-year-old) made her pregnant and she had to have an abortion.'

'Jesus Christ!' I exclaimed. 'No wonder I've been getting strange looks.'

'Well?' June shouted. 'What have you got to say to Jim?'

Annie was blubbering, sucking her bottom lip in and out under her upper one, making a puffing and snorting noise, emphasising the fact that she was very upset. I looked at her with disgust and then as though confiding in her I said softly, 'Shall I tell you what I did to Alice?'

She was immediately silent, the crying stopped and she looked at me expectantly, waiting...

'Sod all!' I bellowed into her face and she recoiled in shock.

There wasn't much we could do; the damage had been done. However, I still got the strange looks and furtive glances. At least, we had consolation in the fact that they weren't hostile enough to be violent. June found that Annie wanted to spend a good deal of her time at the toilets, and that was where she had said all these things. In the end, she was banned from going to the toilets unsupervised. June had to take her, wait while she toileted, showered or whatever and then bring her back.

We went to the Sunday market and as usual, we gave the kids their pocket money so that they could all have a wander round. We usually met at the cafe at a prearranged time. When we met up, Annie had goods way in excess of her pocket money. It wasn't hard to figure out that she had been stealing. When June tackled her about it, she denied it but after some grilling, she broke down and confessed. The evidence was so strong that even she couldn't keep up the pretence. We took her round and made her pay for the items she had stolen and told her we would dock it out of her pocket money. Well, that was it, she couldn't be trusted out of our sight on or off the campsite. It was obvious she couldn't even be sent to do simple chores like fetch a pint of milk; June was lumbered with her. At the start, we had agreed that I should take a back seat as far as the handling of her was concerned. We had learned a big lesson with Alice and would not be easily caught out a second time. Prior to these episodes, Annie had seemed fairly clean; no wet beds or anything like that, but she very quickly transformed her little tent into unbelievable squalor. It absolutely reeked of urine, and shit, everything about it and her, became filthy. Her behaviour had suddenly changed; she was no longer the 'zombie' that we had initially taken in. The strange thing was that her behaviour had altered almost immediately she left the boy's school. At the end of the summer season, we returned home and she started her new school. A permanent social worker had to be assigned to watch and stay with her at all times; this lady found it an almost impossible task. At home, she tried on several occasions to bribe the children with money, in order to get them to come into her room. This came to light very quickly and at a very early stage, we knew that I shouldn't be on my own with her at any time. Her behaviour was such that she had to be taken to school and handed over to the worker who was supervising her. The school would not take responsibility for her at meal times so she had to be collected at lunchtime and taken back. We thought her mental attitude towards younger children was quite odd. She managed to get our neighbour's little girl to drink from a bottle containing hair treatment, and although it was extremely dangerous, luckily the child didn't have to be hospitalised.

We short term fostered two sibling boys and managed to get them a place at the same school as her. On occasions, I took all three of them to school; safety in numbers! One morning her worker didn't turn up at the usual time which meant I would be left on my own with her. So, as we went in, I told the boys to stay with me. We waited for a short time near the headmaster's office, where I usually handed her over to the worker who managed her. The headmaster emerged from his office and upon seeing the boys said: 'What are you boys doing here? You know you're not allowed in the front hall, go on, run along!'

I pointed at the boys and said, 'Stay right where you are!'

Annie's worker arrived almost immediately and I handed her over and dismissed the boys; the headmaster looked shocked.

I said, 'Do you think I could have a word please?'

He opened the door and with his back to it, gestured towards his desk.

'Please, do come in!' He looked questioningly at me.

I said, 'Annie is a sexually abused child. This morning, her care worker didn't arrive at her usual time and the two boys you were going to dismiss were actually chaperoning me.'

He put his hand to his cheek in wonderment, and looking rather puzzled, he said, 'Oh, I see.'

I knew by his attitude that he hadn't the faintest idea what I was talking about. If he had known the agony I had been through for making the mistake of being on my own with another young girl, for a period of around ten seconds, perhaps he could then begin to understand.

During the months that followed, Annie's behaviour became progressively worse. One day, June had a blazing row with her and she stomped her way to her room crying. In an effort to calm her down, June followed her and it was then that she decided to tell June all her troubles. Her sexual abuse started when her mother brought men to the house and they all ended up in bed. Her Mother, her younger brother, herself and the men. This would then turn into a sexual orgy involving all of them. Her mother also played bizarre tricks on the children, one of them being, she smeared tomato ketchup on herself, then laid on the floor screaming. The children dashed in and upon seeing her, became hysterical. She got up laughing, and said it was all a big joke because it was April fool's day.

While she was attending the boy's school, she said she had engaged in sex every day, in the taxi during the journey to and from the school, and at the school. At her previous placements, she had abused all the younger children. This stopped when we went on holiday to Somerset, where June monitored her all the time and almost immediately, her really bizarre behaviour started. Was it frustration? I thought it was. The fact that she was being policed so well, all such activity had stopped and this was her reaction.

The Agency, that placed her with us, arranged for her to have therapy by a lady who came and delved into her problems, and during the initial visit it was decided that she should have a 'safe place' and designated her bedroom. She was to be the only one allowed in there and it very rapidly became just like a rubbish tip. I was dead against such a measure and was absolutely appalled at the mess. As we were passing it, I turned to June and said, 'That room is an absolute disgrace, it's like the Poseidon adventure.'

She had broken the doors off the wardrobe, thrown them across the room, they became lodged partially on her bed, then buried under a mountain of clean and dirty clothes, it was unbelievable. She also threw clothes out of her window into the garden; enough to fill two black bags. When she was confronted with it, she stomped up the stairs, lifting her knees almost to her chin and pounding her foot on each tread with all her might, screeching each time she did it. It was as though she wanted to break every tread. I stood open-mouthed gawking in disbelief. We had no way of disciplining her, she just didn't give a damn what we would do to her, in fact it came over very strongly that she actually wanted physical abuse. I think that was her norm and the environment she seemed to be attempting to create.

June said, 'She wants me to hit her, so it makes me feel as though I have got one over on her when I don't.' Then she gave a little chuckle, but most of the time there wasn't much to laugh about.

It was finally decided that she needed high level therapy. The same Hospital that had dealt with Alice was considered again. I was totally opposed to that idea because of how I thought Alice's case had been mishandled. So, an appointment was set up to see a psychiatrist at a different clinic. The first session we took her to, she completely hoodwinked the lady into believing she was upset at having to go through this sort of ordeal. She sat with her face buried in a cushion, ostensibly sobbing for most of the session. The thing that I found hard to take was: the psychiatrist condoned and even encouraged her by saying, 'Poor Annie, this really has been too much for her.'

When she finally emerged from her cushion, there was neither a tear, nor the trace of a tear.

The psychiatrist said, 'I think what Annie needs, is to be treated like one of your own children, this is where she's missing out, you know.'

I thought that a great deal of thought had gone into her statement.

June said, 'With Annie being sexually abused in the past, that's not possible.'

'Why ever not?' She exclaimed.

'First and foremost, we have the other children's safety to consider and the precautions we have to take, make it impossible for us to do that. For example, there is no way I would want Jim to take her on his knee the way he did with Ellie. I'm afraid that sort of thing could give Annie completely the wrong message.'

'I don't see a problem with that,' she replied.

I glanced at the ceiling. We made absolutely no headway at the meeting. We both thought that this lady hadn't a clue and certainly hadn't got the measure of Annie. Another meeting was set up and they thought it would be of benefit to Annie if these were about a month apart.

Meanwhile, at home and at school, her behaviour became even more difficult and the children said there was a nasty smell coming from her room; Sammy in particular, as his room was next to hers.

'What sort of nasty smell?' I asked.

'Shit,' Sammy said, screwing his face up as if to prevent himself from smelling it.

'What?' I said, surprised.

'Shit!' He said, 'That's the smell!'

One evening, there was an awful commotion upstairs. Sammy was bellowing, 'I'll kill you, you stinking cow.'

When I got there, he was reaching over June attempting to hit her.

'Let me at her!' He sobbed, 'I'll kill the stinking cow.'

I managed to calm him down and he said that he had gone into the bathroom immediately after her and had a shower. When he dried himself, he had got the shit that she had smeared all over the towel, plastered in his hair and on his face.

After that incident, we bought everyone, including us, toilet bags with their own soap, toothpaste, etc. and most important of all, their own towel. That way, there couldn't be a repetition of the smearing. Nothing, not even bottles, soap, toothpaste or any single item was to be left in any of the bathrooms.

Some weeks later, Ellie went into the bathroom after her and started bellowing. This time she had actually done her business in the bath and squeezed it down the plughole. The bathroom stunk to high heaven and I had the unsavoury task of removing it with a sink snake and a plunger.

So, what could we do? June bought a bucket, sponge, cloths and disinfectant. These were to be used to wash the bathroom from top to bottom every time she used it. This helped to satisfy the children, at least the place smelt clean when she had finished her...whatever she got up to.

Life went on and she had her therapy at home which I detested, although I had to agree with June when she said that without the therapist coming and giving her support, she could not have carried on with the placement as long as she did. The bedroom, her 'safe place,' which I thought put us in an impossible situation and resolved nothing, looked more and more as though it had been ransacked by a lunatic burglar and still smelt really unsavoury. We had a couple more meetings at the Hospital. Then they thought it might be beneficial if we went on our own and had a chat, so we agreed; anything was worth a try if it helped the situation. It was a really hot day and the traffic was awful. We virtually cooked on route, at what I thought must have been about gas-mark-5. Upon arrival, the Lady Therapist walked with us to an interview room on the sunny side of the building. When she opened the door, heat billowed out and as we entered, she rushed to open the windows. The temperature was way in excess of a hundred degrees. I rubbed my hands together briskly and joked with a smile, 'Well, that's a bit of luck; at least they've left the heating on for us.'

She turned to face me, and drawing herself up to her full height, she looked down her nose and scornfully asked: 'Do I detect a note of sarcasm? Perhaps you don't want to be here at all?'

My smile faded and I could feel myself bristling although I didn't say anything. We sat through an hour of drivel, about how we should treat Annie as if she were our own daughter; she should be treated the same as the other children.

Finally, I asked, 'Do you think these meetings are beneficial?'

She pondered for several seconds, looked at the ceiling thoughtfully and drummed her fingers lightly on the arm of the chair. 'Yes!' She asserted, looking me straight in the eye.

I looked at June, then at her and said, 'Well, it's a bloody good job one of us does, because I think they're the biggest load of crap I've ever heard in my life.'

There wasn't much more to add after that so we left. I told June that I would not be going back as I thought it was an utter waste of good time. June felt it was her duty to go again and when she did, the meeting was an abysmal failure and she returned home in a hell of a state and vowed never to go again.

It was early morning and the sun was beaming in the window. We were still in bed and I was half asleep when June's voice drifted into my subconscious. 'What are we going to do about this adoption?'

'Yes dear, of course,' I muttered, 'Who are we adopting now?'

She leaned across and gave me a little shake; 'Annie.'

I shot bolt upright. 'What?' I gasped, 'Good grief; I'd sooner adopt Myra Hindley!'

This adoption, the reason she initially came, as far as I was concerned was out of the question. Something would have to be done about it, so we told the adoption agency and agreed to hold her until some alternative could be arranged. If we needed to go anywhere special, that Annie could jeopardise, we were fortunate in that we had a very good friend, Jeannette. She volunteered to take her for the day and even weekends. She was very experienced with disturbed children. I suppose the fact that she had studied as a Nun was a factor in the infinite patience that she appeared to have. Then there was her husband, who had studied to be a priest, he was very easy going. Nothing seemed to ruffle them and the fact that they had adopted several very special needs children made them ideal for the job! After she had been several times, they told us they'd had a blazing row. They had taken the children swimming and Annie had almost drowned their little four-year old girl. Oddly enough they continued to have her, but came to realise just what they were dealing with and were much more vigilant.

Patrick would soon be four, they told us that he would almost certainly never reach the age of two, it had never been known before for a child so severely affected to live beyond that age; he had confounded all the Doctors and experts. The uniqueness of his affliction sparked a lot of interest and the physiotherapist who regularly visited him. She brought several colleagues along and one of them brought a tiny electric wheelchair. The seating area was too large, so they packed it with cushions and tried him in it. He managed to pull the lever which sent it into a spin and that frightened him. Later on, June gently tried him in it again, but this time she operated the lever, and as she moved him around, he began to enjoy it. It wasn't very long before he was driving it himself. He went to each person in turn, stopped at them and then went zooming around the room.

June called anxiously, 'Patrick! No! Stop!' When he went careering into the video recorder. She looked at the others, 'You know what? That's the first time I have said no to Patrick, he's never been naughty before.'

When I arrived home, he was lying on the living room floor on his mat. She smiled and nodded at him. 'Patrick, tell Daddy about your little chair.'

He smiled, 'ZZZZZZZZ' he went, making a whirring sound and flailing his arms to and fro. She said everyone was amazed that he was able to drive the chair. We knew we had to get him a chair and if the DHSS wouldn't provide it, we would have to get it ourselves.

Shortly after this happened, June and Jeannette went with Annie, to an exhibition for the disabled and there it was, large as life on one of the stands, the very same chair that he had driven. He became so excited when he saw it that June asked if he could have a go in it. 'ZZZZZZZZ' he was going, flailing his arms again. Unfortunately, it didn't have any batteries; he didn't mind though; he was happy just to sit in it.

We had an offer from a charity to say if the DHSS turned him down, they would supply the necessary funds. It was imperative that we pressed the DHSS to get a move on, so we made an appointment to see their doctor. The last episode had been too much for June and she said she would not go to see another one of these awful people. I said I was quite happy to take him, and I sat outside the office with Patrick while we were waiting to be seen. He was on his mat, on the floor playing, and I could feel myself getting keyed up, ready for the confrontation that I felt was about to take place. Where did they get these idiots? They were either uncaring, unfeeling or just plain stupid, or perhaps all three. The Doctor called me in and I laid Patrick on his play mat on the bench. He had never seen a child with Patrick's complaint and was very interested. His manner put me at ease immediately and he did a very brief examination. He made a fuss of him and got an instant response and said: 'Of course Patrick needs a wheelchair, that's his basic human right.'

I couldn't believe it, I felt like rubbing my hands with glee. The next stage was to go to another department and choose a chair. We knew exactly what we wanted, but when we got there, they told us that particular chair was not on their list. It would have to be a Bambino, about twice the size. After some very careful consideration, I told June that although he had got on very well with the other one, the Bambino might be more stable, especially if he went out in the garden with it. It had four wheels and would be virtually impossible to capsize. Even though I had never seen the other one, judging by her description, I had reservations, so I coaxed her into accepting this one. Because he was so tiny, it would have to be specially adapted and the whole thing would take a couple of months, but he would be mobile by Christmas. When they showed us the Bambino, I said that he would not be able to manage a gate control, or one that was mounted on the side, and I stressed how important that was. When it came, the controls were 'gate control,' and on the side, there was no way he could possibly reach them. They had given us exactly what we didn't want and as I had predicted, it was utterly useless! We would have to wait until they get their act together and convert it. Now that we had the chair, even though it was useless, the charity that had volunteered to supply the funds, regarded us as already having one. There was nothing we could do and precious hours were ticking away. They came and made up a special seat so that he could fit in it. It was perfect, he could now reach the controls but when he operated them, it lurched backwards and made him panic. There was no way of controlling it, immediately he operated the handle, it got full power and lurched backwards, and made his head flop; there was nothing we could do but wait...

Don.

We were asked to take Don, a ten-year-old boy. He was highly disturbed, in fact I would say in some ways, he even outstripped Annie, so that had to be some sort of a record. He'd only been with us a week or so and I was getting ready to go to the Hospital for one of my regular check-ups, when June, looking rather flustered, rushed into the room.

'Don's gone! The back window is wide open and he's gone!'

'So, what are you going to do?' I asked.

I knew there wasn't much point in running around trying to find him.

'I'm going to phone the police,' she said, 'they'll have to deal with it.' She picked the phone up and dialled.

As she waited to be answered, she held her hand over the mouthpiece and said: 'He was very aggressive and determined; he told me he was going to do it, he stuck his chin out, and scowling at me, he said, 'you can't keep me here, I'm going to run away to my Nan's.'

As she started giving the police details, I whispered, 'I'd better run along.'

She dismissed me impatiently with a wave of her hand, but must have had second thoughts, she kissed her fingertips and touched my cheek.

As I headed down into the town in the minibus, there was some sort of a traffic jam up ahead in the high street, so I joined the queue. Our van as we called it, the Mercedes mini-bus, was quite high and I could see over the top of all the vehicles in front. A police car up front had its blue flashing lights on and was zooming to and fro. It went bumping up the kerb on one side of the road then zigzagged to the other side, all the way down the road, until it ground to a halt partially inside a shop's entrance. Two policemen jumped out and joined several others who were dashing around. The traffic started to filter away and as I came even with several coaches parked opposite, Don came streaking out into the road from between two of them. He was a sight; his face was scarlet, his jaw set in determination. He was running so hard that his jacket had almost slipped off and was hanging inside out from his wrists and flowing horizontally behind him. He was in full flight with two Policemen pursuing him and two others coming from either ends of the coaches. I knew he was about to be apprehended by the long arm of the law.

'Nothing much I can do here,' I told myself. I couldn't help having a little smile when I saw him. He looked not unlike me when I was his age. The same squat build, same colouring and deprived background, complete with built in aggression. Although I found it amusing, it made me feel really sad. I had managed to get out of this circle of depravation, but alas, Don, I feared had no chance. That, I suppose was the reason I found fostering him so traumatic.

The police informed June that he had been picked up and was at the police station. 'What shall we do with him?' They asked.

'Oh!' June said, 'Can you bring him home please? He's got to stay here with us!'

There was silence on the other end for a few seconds: 'I'm sorry, I'm afraid we can't do that, you'll have to come and pick him up!'

She thought that was rather odd, but said she'd be along as soon as I was available.

He was out the back, possibly in the cells and as they brought him in, he was creating an almighty racket, screeching and bawling at them. Despite being so small, it took a lot of effort for the two officers to bring him in and the moment they released him, he squared up to the Sergeant who recoiled in shock.

'Don't you dare try to hit me boy!'

It looked to June as though he was about to hit Don. She was sure that he had never encountered any of these inner London streetwise kids before. If he had hit him, Don would have screamed abuse and all in sundry would have descended to investigate child abuse and Police brutality. The police accompanied us home and June told Don to go and get cleaned up. She smiled knowingly when the Sergeant said he was absolutely horrified, this was his first encounter with a disturbed child of this sort from such a deprived background. He was holding his hands out expressively and shaking his head, as though he didn't believe what had just taken place.

'He kept putting his fists up at me,' he continued, 'You can't keep me here; I'm going to run away to my Nan's, he kept saying, so I told him, that's just where you're wrong son, you have to go back to your Foster parents!'

June said, 'I have to agree, he is particularly difficult, and he does come over as extremely aggressive. He has only just come to us you know; his background is horrendous; drug dealing, stealing and he's only ten years old, it makes you wonder what's to become of him.'

'Well,' said the sergeant, 'I must say I had no idea kids like him even existed. I take my hat off to you, because I know that I couldn't cope with the likes of him; they would drive me crazy.'

June said: 'Well, at least they're not all like this. I suppose he thinks that if he runs away all the time you will have no alternative but to send him back to his Nan's. In a funny sort of way that's quite logical. Any way, he affects his Nan the same way; she can't cope with him and that's why he's here in the first place. She actually asked for him to be taken into care, he was running wild and out of control, so he has to stay here with us because we are experienced in handling very disturbed children.'

They edged their way to the door, and she said her thanks for their trouble and they left. Don hadn't said very much since he returned.

'We're your family now,' June reassured him; 'We'll look after you until you grow up.'

'You're not my family! I don't belong here!' He said, 'I want to be with my Nan; she's my family!'

'But Don, your Nan wants you to stay here...'

Before she could finish, he interrupted saying, 'You're not my family, I don't belong here!'

It was like a recording, every time she said anything he looked into space and droned the same thing, over and over until at one point, he stopped, squinted at her and whispered threateningly: 'I'll make your life so miserable; you'll be glad to send me back to my Nan's.' Then he reverted to his broken record syndrome. She could see that it was utterly pointless and decided to leave it; his Nan and Granddad would be visiting in a day or so.

The next day, I was working at home erecting a shed.

'Why don't you take Don out to help you?' she said, volunteering me and I hesitated at the door.

'You'd like that, wouldn't you Don?' She asked.

He looked from side to side, screwed his mouth up and shrugged. It was clear he didn't give a damn. I waited but he didn't say anything.

'C'mon then mate,' I said cheerfully, 'I could do with some help.'

To my surprise, he got up and came straight away.

'Oh! Don, you'd better put a coat on,' June said, 'It's very cold out there!'

'That's all right,' I said as I went out, 'He can come out when he's ready.'

He turned up, and along with other various tools, I had the drill set up and plugged in. In those days, drills weren't cordless, so it was a big, quite powerful, mains electric one, and having drilled some large holes in the metal, I was screwing nuts and bolts up.

'I'll be with you in a minute,' I smiled, 'I'll just finish this, then we can get started.'

I turned my back and almost immediately the drill went whirr, whirr, whirr.

I swung round and put my hand up in a stop sign. 'Careful Don! If that catches your clothes or your gloves, it'll injure you.'

I waited a few seconds, he was still holding onto it, so I patted the air with my hand in a stop sign and pointed my index finger skywards. 'Just put it down please and don't touch it! That's a good boy.'

Very slowly, he put it down.

'Good boy.' I reassured him and turned my back.

'Whirr' the drill went again, instantly followed by a shriek. I turned in time to see him drop the drill to the ground and clutch his left hand; and I thought I could see blood.

'What the...' I gasped, 'Are you alright?'

His face was contorted in agony. I took hold of his hand, and said: 'Here, let's have a look.

The palm of his glove was completely shredded. Fortunately, his hand was only grazed.

'I think you'd best go indoors and get a dressing on that.' I said and ushered him towards the house. June was very concerned, even though she said it was a minor cut.

I took her to one side and said, 'I think he didn't believe me when I said the drill would injure him, so he tried it on his glove. He's lucky his glove took most of it; I don't want him around me again when I've got any tools out.'

She shook her head and gave a little, 'Shush.'

His Nan and Granddad came a few days later and during the course of their visit, he tortured her mentally until she was in such a distressed state that she was a blubbering wreck.

'They're not my family, I don't belong here; I want to go home with you.' He repeated it hundreds of times.

'You know the Council won't allow you home with us while we are in that flat.' She sobbed again and again. 'We're doing all we can, they said we could have a bigger place; a house, then you would be able to come home.'

'Poor woman' I thought, 'She can't face him with the truth.'

When we first agreed to take him, they told us that she just couldn't cope. She had become so frustrated that she was battering him regularly and on occasions had knocked him to the floor and jumped up and down on him. The alternative to us was a lock up, similar I suppose, to what they had in mind for Terry.

I went into the kitchen where June was making tea and I said: 'I'm absolutely fed up listening to that kid. They're not my family,' I mimicked, 'he's said it so often; look at the state of his Nan! I reckon if he went back to her, they'd have to cart her off to a home for the bewildered.

June squinted threateningly at me, as though I was a naughty boy, and said: 'Stop it!' With that, someone opened the door; it was Don.

'Tea's just coming,' she said cheerfully and we went back into the living room. They left shortly afterwards and although she'd had a hard time, she managed to convince him that it was not in his best interest to run away again. That would make life a little bit more bearable, knowing that at least he had a little bit of stability.

One of his main problems was that he was a chronic bed wetter; the worst we'd ever encountered! Because he was so heavy and just could not be roused, June was unable to lift him at nights, so it meant that I had to do the honours. He went to bed around eight thirty, nine o'clock, and I lifted him at ten thirty but by that time, he was invariably saturated right up to and below his pillow, meaning an entire bed change, sheets and even the pillow; thank God for rubber sheets! I usually left the second lift until I was about to go to bed at around twelve, and we always had a repeat performance. The strange thing was, when I lifted him, despite the fact that he was drenched, he still, in his zombie like state, managed each time to do a wee. On many occasions, he would come into our room in the mornings and June seeing a different pair of pyjamas on him would say, 'Did you have an accident last night?'

Nodding affirmatively, he said: 'But I've changed my bedding.'

The first time he said it I couldn't believe my ears. When he left the room, I nudged her. 'That's three lots last night; he's unbelievable.'

She just shook her head, 'Sometimes I get four off him; it doesn't matter.'

We took the children to a fun park with swimming and boating. They took their rubber dingy and set off together to the canal; it was all quite safe, so we relaxed. They came back later, dragging the boat and laughing at the fun they'd had. Don was looking really happy for a change, and said: 'That was brilliant!'

Smiling, June asked, 'Did you enjoy that?'

They all chorused together how good it was.

'Are you happy then Don?' She asked.

He was grinning broadly, 'Ye...' he didn't finish the word, his smile vanished and squinting at her, with real venom in his voice, he said: 'No! I'm not! And you know why.'

It really brought home how disturbed he was, when Annie said, 'Don needs a psychiatrist.' I thought that was pretty rich coming from her. She didn't like him much anyway. The day he arrived he dropped her in it. She came up behind him, bent over and kissed him. 'Have you ever had sex?' She said provocatively.

'Why, have you?' He asked.

'Yes!' She said, 'with my mum's boyfriends, my brother and some boys at school.'

He immediately told June what she had said. He wasn't being a good boy, that was his way of being nasty, and she just happened to be the first one to give him ammunition. It was not the start of a beautiful friendship because she was on punishment straight away.

As it was summer holidays once again, we bought him a tent so he could be on his own. The other children refused point blank to have him in their tent, not that we would have put him in there anyway. My work situation, not to mention finances, wouldn't allow me to have the six weeks off. June assured me that she could cope with the children, so reluctantly I agreed to leave her in Somerset with them. I did feel sceptical because, as well as our own kids, she had Patrick, Annie and Don. Each one on their own enough for any normal woman to manage, but then, I had figured out years earlier that she was definitely not ordinary. No news was good news, I had heard nothing and felt that I could safely assume that all was well. I finished late on Friday, so was unable to go straight after work. I went late-night shopping, got the week's groceries and left very early the next morning. It was a lovely sunny morning and when I arrived, I was met by our friend Connie who was also very experienced with special needs children.

She said, 'June is not feeling so good.'

I felt panic rising, 'What's wrong, are the children okay?'

'Oh, they're okay. It's Don, he's really been a little... swine.'

I was shocked to see June. I had never seen her like this before. She was in a similar state to Don's Nan when he had mentally tortured her.

'I'll be all right,' she sobbed, 'I really don't know what's come over me; I'm just a bit depressed.'

Don had run away leaving her on the beach with the other children. Joe was working on the markets and bought a Peter Powel kite. He was getting on really well with it, so Don went and bought one, but when he found he couldn't master it, he sent it crashing into Joe's deliberately, resulting in the destruction of both. He had this thing about Joe, he was around the same age and the same size, and when he first came to us, I was going into the living room and they came out of the back room. Joe was in front and looked quite relaxed but Don, following, looked all sweaty and scarlet.

'What's going on?' I enquired.

Joe jerked his thumb over his shoulder at him and said: 'He wants to have a bundle all the while, but he's no good at it.'

I did my best to keep a straight face and carried on into the room.

As if our task wasn't difficult enough, his Nan gave him fifty pounds for his holidays, would you believe? Not for us to shell out to him over the period we were going to be there, but directly to him. This of course did wonders for the relationship between him and the other children; I suppose they felt like the poor relations. Who in their right mind gives a highly disturbed ten-year-old boy fifty quid just like that? I could not comprehend her logic!

At home, his bedding was not a problem, or perhaps I should say it was a problem but at least there, June was able to manage it; with great difficulty. Here however, where facilities and amenities were so limited, it was a monumental chore, which when added to all the other problems, made it an unbearable burden. I listened to her for quite some time and the thing that struck me in all of this was: Annie had faded into oblivion; she wasn't even mentioned, nor was Patrick.

Finally, June, looking up, wiped her eyes and sobbed, 'I'll be alright, don't worry!'

I looked at Connie and said, 'What do think about all this then?'

She put her hand on June's knee and in an affectionate way, gave her a little shake, and talking more to June than me, she said, 'She'll be all right, she's just going through a bad patch.'

I looked out of the caravan window, and I could see Don, strutting around with his hands deep in his pockets, scowling at the grass and occasionally kicking it in an aggressive manner. I drew a deep breath, slapped my hands on my knees and stood up. 'Right then,' I said, 'Shall I tell you what I think?'

I looked enquiringly from one to the other. They didn't say anything so I pointed out the window at Don. 'Do you see that little monster out there? Well, take him out of your life and it will revert to some sort of normality. Now, in a minute, I'm going to go and phone Out-of-Hours and ask to have him removed at the earliest possible moment!'

I waited to see what sort of protest she was going to make, to my surprise she didn't. I felt sure she was relieved that I had taken the initiative. When I got through, I could feel myself bristling; the Out-of-Hours Social Worker on duty was Ronald. I hadn't seen or spoken to him since the debacle with Alice. He told me that as it was a holiday weekend, it would be Tuesday before they could pick him up, because they also needed to find an alternative placement.

'Are you happy with that?' He asked.

There was nothing on this earth that Ronald could ever have done that would make me happy, I absolutely despised this man, but I agreed, if Tuesday was the earliest, then that would have to do. I told him to make sure not to send just one person, I was not certain how Don would react, very possibly how he did when he first came to us. Thinking he would react in the way that a child would when he was being rejected. We prepared ourselves for the worst and decided to tell him that he was going to be removed. We needn't have bothered, he didn't turn a hair, in fact he seemed overjoyed at the prospect. I planned on staying until they fetched him. I wanted to protect June as much as possible.

It was very early morning; we had just got up and I heard someone moving about in the awning. The children knew we didn't allow them in there before we were up and about. I looked through the window, it was Don!

'Get out of the awning!' I called.

'No! And you can't make me!' He snarled.

'We'll soon see about that,' I said and as I stepped towards the door, June lunged in front of me, and standing with her back to it, she spread her arms to prevent me from getting out. 'No! No!' She cried, 'Please don't do it!'

She thought I was about to go and batter him, but the thought hadn't entered my head, although I have to admit that when he first came, he did manage to make me feel as though I wanted to. I had to make a conscious effort to mentally 'back off,' and as soon as I did, he never affected me again.

'Don't be silly June!' I said and eased her out of the way.

He was sitting in one of the camping chairs, glowering defiantly at me. I unzipped the awning, picked the chair up with him on it, walked outside and shook him off as though tipping a cat off it.

He turned and glared at me.

'See,' I smiled, 'That wasn't so painful, was it?'

He squinted and clenched his fists at me. I waited a second, and setting the chair down, I copied him. I was smiling inwardly as I lunged towards him. I guess he took me seriously because he took flight as fast as he could go. When he looked back and saw that I wasn't giving chase, I held my stomach with one hand and patted my open mouth with the other, feigning silent laughter and that actually got a smile from him. I went back to the caravan.

'And just what did you think I was going to do?' I said mockingly.

She shook her head, 'I don't know.'

When the Social workers came to collect him, I thought he might create. He didn't, in fact, he went as though they were taking him for a fun day out. They told us that he was going to one of the units in Kent. I had my reservations about all of these so-called 'units.' It seemed to me that when you get a group of disturbed kids together, the very devil couldn't watch them. My fears were well founded, we heard shortly afterwards that he ran away and while he was 'on the run,' stole a motorbike, wrote it off and broke into several shops, presumably to get money to finance him. But then, he ran away when he was with us, so who's to know what the circumstances were. The last we heard was that he did return to his Nan, so perhaps things did work out; who knows? I was quite surprised that we received the information on the motor bike episode. I suppose it would be nice to get reports about children, but then again, so often in a lot of cases, these kids go on a downward spiral, would we really be pleased to get information like that?

Ellie had met a very nice boy and was going steady. I was sitting at the table when June came and stood beside me and said, 'it's Ellie, she's having a baby.'

I was shocked and distressed. I could feel tears welling up and was immediately worried that the baby wouldn't be wanted. Memories of the early days when we took in the young unmarried mothers came flooding back. I swore then that if ever a daughter of mine got pregnant, she would never go through anything like that.

'That's not a problem,' I said shaking my head.

June clasped my head to her bosom. 'It's not the end of the world.'

'I know.'

'At least she'll have our support, won't she?'

'Um hmm.' I muttered. I really didn't feel like a drawn-out conversation, we were talking about a new life here. How easily one just springs forth, 'what will it be for him or her?'

Many years earlier, we had all joined in a demonstration with SPUC, the Society for the Protection of the unborn Child, so abortion was a course of action that we would never have considered, and we thought that Ellie felt the same. As time wore on, I became really excited at the idea of having my first Grandchild, and Ellie was keen to have this baby, and by all accounts, so was her boyfriend.

Paul.

June saw Paul, an eleven-year-old boy advertised in a magazine as needing a family and she said: I saw a television program highlighting him, when he was just seven.'

She said how awful it was that he had been left to drift in the system for four years. He was profoundly deaf with no speech, of African parents and very black. We knew we would have problems because of the political criteria laid down by our authority. They insisted on placing like with like, hence they needed a black, Rastafarian, deaf, or at least deaf signing family. I laughed and said that they would be as likely to find a family like that on the moon, but then, the authorities at that time, seemed to me to put their criteria way above the actual needs of the child. If they couldn't get what they considered to be correct, or politically correct, then the child invariably got nothing, and that was exactly what Paul got for over four years. That's what spurred us on to apply, if we hadn't, I am certain he would have continued to drift and would have been lost in the system.

Quite some time later, after we adopted him, and at one point, June, along with Paul and Sammy, was on television talking about our fostering and adoption experiences, and that was quite nice.

Anyway, the one exception to their politically correct rules seemed to be ourselves. Us being Northern Irish Protestants, were placed time and again, Southern Irish Catholic children. Because we were a large Irish family, I assume that everyone thought we had to be Catholics, so no one ever bothered to check. It seemed to me that their criteria were strictly reserved for the slightest degree of colour, and that was the reason Paul had been held back; what a waste of a young life! We applied, were assessed and the wheels went into motion. If he was going to be placed, it would be absolutely essential for us to have deaf signing lessons, so we were assigned Bill, a social worker who came every Saturday morning. He was a really nice teacher, and we all thoroughly enjoyed it. As she predicted, June was the dunce in the class, with even the little ones taking the mickey. I have to admit that despite having had deaf friends as a youth and had learned the alphabet and a few other bits and pieces, I was running a close second. Annie, who I thought would be an absolute duffer, was doing extremely well, much better than us.

Social Services arranged a visit to a lady in Nottingham who was something of an authority on deaf children, having adopted two. We eagerly agreed to have a weekend away, just the two of us, and Patrick; it certainly was a weekend to remember. Her twin boys were around twelve, very black, rubella damaged, profoundly deaf and really bizarre. One of them did weird dances, pivoting and gyrating around us and when he wasn't doing that, he tore magazines into strips and posted them into a box. Meanwhile the other one, tore carrier bags into strips, twisted the strips so that they looked like pieces of string, made loops with them and holding them like a magnifying glass gave us the Sherlock Holmes treatment. Tea was like the mad-hatter's tea party, with them contesting for each other's seat, or running through the house, then dashing back, leaping over the table into the seats at the back and bellowing at each other. The lady was lovely, with infinite patience. I knew there and then that I could not possibly cope with the boy we were about to take if he was anything like this. She had moved them out of their room temporarily in order to accommodate us. That was all very nice until about 5.00am. They came in, one after the other, then several times during the course of the morning. Each time they signed the same question, 'Where's Mummy?'

I pointed at the ceiling indicating that she was upstairs. They went out of the door and presumably up the stairs but returned shortly afterwards to ask the same question. This continued until around 8.45 am.

Knowing that there was a question mark over the boy we were about to take; was he rubella damaged? This weekend did not bolster my confidence at all and that coupled with the problem of deaf signing was very worrying, but we decided to press on in any case. Bill, the Social Worker was an old boy, 'Older than me,' I thought. Every Saturday we had our usual pantomime and the signs for 'Happy Birthday' cropped up. Mime clapping hands, 'Happy,' hold your index finger up and blow it as though extinguishing a candle, spread your hands, palms upwards, 'Birthday' and then say your date of birth.

When it came to my turn Bill was surprised.

'We are the same age, even born on the very same day,' he said.

'My Goodness, not twins? The gruesome twosome no less,' I laughed.

The kids laughed and I felt that our relationship was quite special after that.

While all this was going on, we were still coping with Annie. I felt that it was impossible for her behaviour to deteriorate, but it did! The children complained that when they passed her room, the stench was worse; we were still not entering her bedroom. I hated the whole scenario; just to glance in as I passed to go to the bathroom, made me seethe. It looked like the 'Poseidon Adventure part two,' assuming of course that part two would be worse than part one. We were quite desperate to end this saga. They said they were working very hard to find a suitable place for her and we continued to hold her, as it was termed.

We began to wonder if Ellie was pregnant at all, she looked absolutely normal. I was over the moon when she had her baby - Antony and I just adored him. I got our old home movies out one night and one was titled; 'June bathing Sammy.' Everyone gasped at the resemblance. Isn't it strange how time erodes the memory? They looked identical.

Paul arrived and we felt as though we had been thrown in at the deep end. We very soon discovered that he was not as bad as the twins in Nottingham, but had to be a close second. We warned him that under no circumstances was he to go anywhere near Annie's room, and surprisingly, he never did. What he did do was, he barged into everyone else's room unannounced. Ellie became very irate on numerous occasions and June ended up dressing with her backside against the bedroom door. His other trick was to wander around at five in the mornings, switching all the lights on. On one of these episodes, June confronted him on the stairs and told him to go to his bedroom. He sat on the stairs and refused to move. She racked her brain. 'What shall I do with this kid? If I try to manhandle him back into his room, I know I shall lose, he's bigger than me. I can't leave him to wander around waking everyone up.'

She signed to the best of her ability, 'If you don't go back to your bedroom, we shall sit here all day, but there will be no food.' To her surprise that got an immediate response. 'That's how to get to him,' she thought.

He had a thing about orange juice. If he couldn't have orange juice, he would drink nothing. He told us he was allergic to milk and we believed him, until he took a fancy to rice pudding and cream. He would cross his hands, place them on his chest and say in his sign language, 'I love dogs.'

After several attempts at reading his signs, we finally interpreted, 'Can I walk the dog?'

We didn't think that would be a problem, so we let him take our little Jack Russell for a walk, on the lead, down our quite long garden. He broke into a run with her in tow and she ended up barking continuously and skidding along on her back behind him. Everyone was bellowing at him to stop but of course he couldn't hear. He carried on running with me dashing after and trying to catch him. After a few disastrous incidents we banned him from touching the dogs. We made rules; if you touch the dogs, no orange that day, or if you barge into Ellie's, or anyone else's room, no orange! At one stage, he was to have no orange for three days and we were shocked to find that he drunk nothing. So, we made another rule, if he is not allowed orange on a particular day, he would have to drink water instead or he would get no orange the next day. He had to be monitored at all times. We found that he would drink black coffee but not without the proviso, if he didn't drink it; no orange!

He had to be told a time to wake up and would come barging into our room at that predetermined time every morning and that infuriated me. In the end, we made him stay in his room until we told him it was time to get up. It took us over a year to achieve that, mainly by threatening, bed early, or go and stay in his room for ten minutes. He hated staying in his room, he would cry and mimic a yawn, patting his mouth with his hand, the deaf sign for boring. He timed these periods to the second. If he didn't stay in his room for the designated time or go to bed when he was told...no orange!

We were glad we hadn't abandoned ship in the first few weeks which we nearly did.

June said after the first few days, 'I'll never be able to cope with this loopy kid.'

He kept hopping around on his toes, bellowing at the dogs and the children. We had Ellie's dog at the time and thought how nice it would be if we took them and him, out in the van to a nearby park. It was near a road with a considerable amount of traffic. June said it would be much safer if she put all three dog's leads on while we were still in the van, then get them all out together. As she emerged, he spotted a car coming and started bellowing. The dogs, not being used to this, panicked and ran every which way. She ended up doing pirouettes across the field with the dogs milling around her and him yelling at them to stop. The more he yelled the worse they became. I fell out of the van laughing and it took me quite a few minutes to release her from the tangled leads.

'God bless us woman, you look like Gulliver,' I giggled as I untied her.

When we arrived home, Bill was on the phone and June said, 'The thing that I find so hard is the noise he makes.'

'Ah well,' he said, 'I'm afraid that's something you'll have to get used to, that's one of the things about deaf people, they are very noisy.'

As they were to arrange a special School for him, Bill came for the first time since he'd been placed. Paul was making his usual racket, bellowing, snorting and chattering.

'God almighty!' Bill gasped. 'Is he always as noisy as this?'

June said, 'That's what I've been telling you.'

'They won't put up with that at School, that's not normal, he sounds like a chimpanzee.'

We laughed and June said, 'That's not politically correct.'

So, we made another rule; if he is noisy, no orange!

He went to the special school for the deaf for assessment and was immediately rejected. They couldn't cope with him and described him as unmanageable. For the next nine months, we were stuck with him at home, while School and Social Services worked out a plan similar to Annie's, where he would have a full time Support Worker.

The Wheelchair.

Social workers came to make sure Patrick was going to go to school. He couldn't sit up, stand, walk or talk, and was particularly vulnerable to infections. On one occasion, while June was in the same room attending to another child, a toddler who came to his birthday party, dragged him off the settee by his hair. He was on the floor before June could get to him, what chance would he have in a class full of children?

'They make me sick, working on their idiotic theories. The first thing we will know is, he will get 'flu' off one of them and that will be the end of him.' I said angrily and pointed at Paul, 'Why the hell don't they do something about a school for him?'

June tutted impatiently, 'For goodness' sake Jim, they are just doing their job.'

'Well, are you going to send him to school?'

She adjusted her glasses and gave a little chuckle. 'No, I'm not! But I'll be a bit more subtle about it than you.'

Patrick still hadn't got his new wheelchair sorted. We had made numerous phone calls and applications about it to no avail. His lifestyle could have been so different during these wasted months. We had all sorts of excuses, until finally, they said it was just not possible to do what we wanted; these wheelchairs are not meant for that sort of control. June got in touch with the makers of the wheelchair to see if there was anything they could do, but their technician was not available, he was due back from holiday shortly. A couple of days later, I received a call from the technician.

'Could we come to the factory? Please bring the wheelchair and be sure to bring Patrick!'

Movement at last! We couldn't believe it, we were like kids waiting for Christmas, which incidentally was about two weeks away, so the useless wheelchair had been sitting for over a year. On the day of the visit, the three of us plus Paul arrived. They still hadn't sorted his school out, so, where we went, he went. It was quite a large factory, crisp and clean. We were welcomed as though we were all important, and Patrick? Well, no one had ever treated him as though he was the main attraction before, even though we always felt that he was. They sat him in his wheelchair and did some expert calculations.

'I'm afraid this will take a little time,' the Engineer said. 'Come, I will show you round the factory while they make up the framework!'

I thought, 'They've dropped everything to deal with Patrick, a bit different to the DHSS rubbish.'

As we walked around, I knew instantly why Patrick was important. There were quite a few disabled people working in the factory. Patrick's chair was in pieces in one of the work bays and a workman said to the engineer, 'the bearings are all shot in this, I'll have to put new wheels on it.'

I was more than surprised, because it had supposedly been fully serviced by the DHSS before they delivered it, and so far, it hadn't been used!

The Engineer gave a little wave, dismissing the problem, 'Anything it needs; do it!'

He showed us the control Patrick's chair would have. 'This is just like any joystick,' he said manoeuvring it around in his hand. 'Forward and you go forward, backwards for backward and so on. This is the dearest part of it, and it is quite fragile. It is good for something like a million operations, or one drop.'

We got to the end of our tour and he looked at his watch. 'I guess we shall be another half hour or so. If you'd like to nip off for some lunch, hopefully everything will be ready when you return, then we can give this little man his test flight,' he said as he shook Patrick's hand.

When we returned, they were all set and waiting, the Engineer, the Mechanic and the Electrician. They put him in the chair and made a few adjustments. Patrick didn't seem to want to participate. I suppose he remembered how it had jolted when it had the old useless gate control. After a little while, he pulled the joystick and went backwards.

'That's his main sort of action,' I said, 'He has a problem pushing things, he always seems to want to pull.'

'Is that so?' He looked the electrician: 'Can you wire this so that when he pulls, it will go forward?'

'Hmm,' he said nodding, 'That's not a problem.'

Within a few minutes, Patrick was driving around very gently and gradually got more daring as we encouraged him. The more we called to him to go this way or that, the more attention it seemed to create and when I looked around, I was surprised to see the entire workforce had come to see him perform; it was wonderful! As we were leaving, they showed us a bulletin board with pictures of disabled people who had been 'kitted out' by the factory and asked if we would mind sending a photograph of Patrick. June said we would love to. We were overwhelmed by the reception, the treatment, the patience and the outcome; it could not have been better. Everyone was so excited at how Patrick's life, in a few short hours had been transformed. He couldn't drive it backwards to start with. Everyone kept telling him, 'Back! Back!' When he finally did, he kept careering around the living room shouting, 'Back! Back!' That was the only word he actually mastered.

Things were pretty hectic coming up to Christmas, with the shopping and generally running around, we were glad it was over. It gave us a lot more time to spend with Patrick. His skill with his wheel chair had improved and the better he became at it, the naughtier he became. We were watching him crash into the furniture and shout; 'back! Back!' then go zooming off backwards.

'Look at that bloody little imp,' I laughed as I nudged her. 'Can you not control your child?'

'Patrick! You naughty boy! What are you doing?' She laughed.

He just kept giggling and flying round the room. I hadn't got a video camera, just an ancient relic of an eight-mm sound movie camera that I had kept from the old days when the kids were little. I said I would make a special effort and get some films for it to take movies of him, but that evening, we were invited to Antony's paternal grandparents for supper. It was an evening out for us with the little ones. The big ones had other things to do but it wouldn't be much as they all had stinking colds, Sammy in particular.

I thought at the time how odd it was that it seemed to affect just the teenagers.

We took Patrick's wheelchair and had a really nice evening. The kids were excellent, all except Patrick; naughty little rascal! Every time we gave him a biscuit or a cake, he ate half and the other half whizzed across the room. June was very apologetic, 'this wheelchair has really turned him into a little hooligan,' she laughed.

Towards the end of the evening, I noticed that he was sweating profusely. This was one of the things about his disability; his thermostat was a bit up the creek.

'I'll take him over near the door where it's a bit cooler,' I said manoeuvring his chair round the room. I took his cardigan off and he seemed to stabilise but June thought it would be best if we went home.

Nursing him in the car as she normally did, she said, 'This little man is not very well you know,' as she put her hand on his forehead. 'He's got a temperature.'

'We'll be home in a minute,' I reassured her.

Farewell to Patrick.

I was getting the children off to bed, when June came out of the living room, mopping herself down with a tissue and looking rather flustered, said. 'Patrick's just been sick everywhere.'

'Do you think he'll be okay?' I asked.

'I don't like it; I think I'd better sleep downstairs with him tonight. I'll give him something but it won't do a lot of good if he can't keep it down.'

She had learned early on to act immediately on the slightest sign of infection. Septrin was what he normally had for sniffles and slight colds, but she always had other medication as emergency standby. If she hadn't, he would probably have gone when the doctors predicted.

In the morning, I took a cup of tea in to her and she said, 'I'm worried Jim, I'm going to call the Doctor.'

He gave us a letter to the Hospital and said, 'Take him over straight away, they don't object to mothers staying in with their babies.'

Even though he was over five, he was the size of a one-year-old and still our little baby. The nursing Staff had never seen a child with Patrick's complaint before, so he created quite a stir and was immediately put on antibiotics. June stayed with him and I went home to see to the others. When I returned, she was trying to give him a bottle; he had never outgrown the baby stages. I took his big toe and gave it a little squeeze, shaking it gently I said: 'Hello Paddy Paddy,' he beamed his usual smile.

'Is he a lot better?' I asked hopefully.

She swallowed hard and looked as though she was going to cry.

'The Sister asked me just how far I was prepared to go with this baby,' she said almost inaudibly. I felt an invisible band tighten round my heart when she said: 'I told her I am prepared to do whatever is necessary, I haven't brought him here to die.'

A nurse came in and gave him some pink medicine. 'At least he's managed to keep this down,' June said as she mopped his mouth.

I stayed as long as I could but left to attend to the others. When I returned, they had been moved into a little side ward near the entrance. It was very warm and he had only a nappy on. When I tugged his toe, and did my usual, 'hello Paddy Paddy.' He didn't respond and I felt alarmed. We sat by his bedside and he drifted off. The nurse came in and did her checks. She gently roused him and gave him his pink medicine and checked his drip. The big ones had agreed to look after the little ones so I was able to stay quite some time. Hours later, the nurse came in again, checked him and gave him some more medicine. I felt an icy hand grasp my heart when it just trickled out of his mouth.

'Oh God, he's dying' I told myself but didn't say anything to June.

The nursing staff arrived with an assortment of machinery, an oxygen tent which they set up and a little light on his toe that monitored him. During all of this, Patrick didn't stir. They set up a machine that gave two digital readouts, one for oxygen and one for the pulse and told us what the readouts should be; they fluctuated wildly.

'At least now, he'll have a chance to respond,' Sister said, 'he will get his antibiotics intravenously, so he won't sick them up.'

I had to go back home again. When I was about to return to the hospital, several of the children wanted to come too. There was no change but while we were there, the numbers on the monitor reeled wildly up and down and the alarm bells went off. The nurse came running, hastily adjusted everything and he seemed to stabilise.

June ushered me to one side and said, 'Patrick is dying, so we had better prepare ourselves for the worst. He's not responding to any of the treatment.'

I stared at the floor and shook my head. I knew she was right and I had known for some time. Jeannette, our friend, who had given us respite with Annie, turned up at the hospital. Her friend's baby was ill in the same ward. She called in to see us and sat for a long time and we talked about the possible outcome.

'What do you want from Patrick?' She asked, analysing me.

I said, 'I don't want anything from him! I've loved him all his life and all I want now is to love him at his time of death; to be here if he needs me.'

Jeannette left and as I got up to go, I said to June, 'One of the loves of his life was his music, when I come back next time, I'm going to bring some tapes with me and I'll put them close to his ear, I want him to know we are here.'

David and his girlfriend turned up and also Ellie and her boyfriend. The little ward was practically full. I expected Sister to create when she turned up but she didn't, she was amazed and said she had never witnessed anything like this before. With everyone present, it meant that June could take a break; she hadn't slept for days. I took some of the children home and gathered his favourite tapes to take back. Some of Sammy's friends had come to the house to see him; he had been ill for some time.

'I've got a virus,' he sobbed, 'And now I've given it to my little brother and he's in hospital dying.'

When I returned, Carol and Jackie, our old faithful friends were there; the ward was virtually full again. I shook my head, 'No change then?'

June pointed at the monitor, 'That keeps going up and down, it's about twenty up at the minute. The nurse turned the alarm bell off because she was in and out of here like a yoyo.'

I pulled a chair up beside the bed and switched his music on. The figures on the monitor settled and stabilised instantly.

'My word!' I said, 'did you see that? Well at least he knows we're here.' I could feel tears welling up and a lump in my throat. 'I don't want him to die, not if there's a ghost of a chance.'

June took my hand and squeezed it. 'I know love, but you won't have to care for him. If he gets better, I'll never know anything but fear, I'll be afraid to take him anywhere in case he gets sick.'

'You go and get some sleep!' I said, 'David and I will watch over him.'

We watched him for two days, covering the opening in the oxygen tent to keep the numbers stable. Carol ferried the children to and fro; she was a gem.

The strange thing was, during the two-day vigil, on the occasions that June took over, the numbers on the monitor went crazy. Even in his coma, he seemed to know; so, she took a back seat. On the afternoon of the fourth day. Carol, June and I were the only ones there when two Ministers from our church came in.

'The Reverend Brown is away at the moment,' they told us.

We gathered round the bed in a little group and said prayers. Were they meant to comfort us? Help Patrick? I just didn't know. What they did, was make me feel dreadful and highlight the fact that he was doomed.

On the fifth day, we told everyone that they should go and get cleaned up. June had as good a rest as was possible under the circumstances. She assured me that she would be okay, she'd manage. Carol stayed on and I left. Strolling to the car, I just couldn't rush. I drove slowly home deep in thought and as I arrived, Carol was coming out of our house. 'She's a sweetie,' I thought, 'she's obviously been checking up to see that the kids are okay.'

I smiled as she approached.

'Jim,' she said and hesitated for a few seconds and put her hand on my forearm. 'Patrick died, not five minutes after you left. It was as though he wanted to be on his own with June.'

I knew it had been inevitable but it didn't alter the fact that I felt dreadful. I looked right through her and said, 'I'll have to go and tell Ellie! She won't know.'

I drove to Ellie's place in a daydream, she smiled when she opened the door and taking her in my arms I said, 'I'm sorry darling,' 'Patrick died at five to five.'

She was hugging me and howling, I could feel her shaking in my arms. It made me feel so impotent; there was nothing I could do to take her pain away. I knew she would feel it really bad as she had done so much of the caring for him.

'I'm going back over to the hospital now, your Mum's over there on her own.'

When I arrived, Carol and Jackie were already there. June had dressed him in a baby grow. His trials of life were over, he looked relaxed now. She hugged me as soon as I walked in and said, 'it's all over now, he won't suffer any more. You hadn't gone more than a few minutes when the pulse reading on the monitor suddenly plummeted to zero and before I could call the nurse, the oxygen dropped to zero. The nurse came straight away and started to examine him. I took hold of the tubes and said, "Get this rubbish off him, he's dead! I want to dress him! I don't want him lying around like this," and she dismantled it all.'

Ellie and Derek turned up with Antony. He and Patrick had been such good pals. They had whizzed around on his wheelchair together with Patrick driving just a week ago.

'Patrick sleeping,' he said and gently tapped his eyes.

'Yes darling,' June said and he resumed playing his little game.

Patrick looked tinier than ever, the week's illness had drained what little resources he had and left him with virtually nothing. I wanted to give him a last cuddle, so I took him on my knee and stroked his hair. I touched his nose and to my amazement, it was soft. When he was alive, I would do this, tap his nose or cheek. He always responded by giving his little laugh and tapping the same number of times. However, due to his rare condition, he had little fat cheeks and stubby nose that had the texture of flexed muscle, as though they were pumped up. All the tension was gone, he was relaxed.

When the sister came in, June said she wanted to wrap him up and take him home.

'Oh! No no no no my dear, you can't do that!' She said, 'he has to be taken to the morgue and the death has to be registered in the morning! Then the body can be released to the undertakers.'

So that was it, he was dead and gone. I could remember so clearly my words to June when he was laughing: 'Do you know what? This little man has got so little in life, yet he gives so much; he's a little magic man.'

He'd had so little and such a short time. The only consolation was he'd had us. We hoped he had been lucky because of that, we knew that we were the lucky ones to have had the privilege of him, the Gods had really smiled on us when they sent him to us.

So, he went to the morgue and we went home to plan the funeral. These were sad days for us, the little light that had shone so brightly had faded and gone out. I wondered if ever there would be a happy time for us again, and even now, when I read this, all these years later, the sadness and the heartache come flooding back.

June went to the undertakers, dressed him in his brand-new suit, did his hair which everyone admired and finally, hooked his dummy on his finger that he always had when he was alive; one in his mouth, and the one on his finger that he would sling across the room if he wanted anything. This time though, she had to make do with the one on his finger. I went to see him and found it so difficult to suppress the tears; I touched his cheek.

'He feels so cold,' I sighed to Joe whom I had brought with me; he was sobbing.

Later on, June said, 'Jim, it's really strange, but when I dressed Patrick, he had been cut open and they had sewed him up with a bit of string; just like a potato sack, it made me feel awful.'

I couldn't volunteer any information as to why that should be, but I found that very distressing too. We had promised to send photos of Tim to the place that had done his wheelchair, we'd had a photographer come in and do the honours. I made a special effort the day after he died and wrote a letter to the people who had been so kind and they phoned; it must have been as soon as he received my letter.

We told everyone that we didn't want flowers but would be grateful for a donation to the society who had been supportive during his life. With Patrick being a Catholic, we wanted him to have a Catholic service at the funeral, but we also wanted our Minister, who had taken such an interest in his welfare and done so much for him, to assist as well if that was possible. I befriended some priests at a Priory where I had done a lot of work and thought how nice it would be if they could perform the ceremony as they had known Patrick personally. We were delighted when everyone agreed to take part just as we had hoped.

A few days later, David stayed the night and was leaving for work at around six a.m. when Terry, came up the garden with a friend.

Terry said, 'David will give us a lift home! Won't you David?'

David was so surprised at seeing them that he was lost for words.

'Err' he stammered, 'Yeah, alright! The car's open, just get in and I'll be along in a minute!'

He went indoors to collect his bag and when he got in, they were already on board in the back. Terry was absolutely blotto and laughing drunkenly about some manor house, where they had got 'pissed up,' as he called it. David stopped outside Terry's house and was shocked when they unloaded TV's and videos. He didn't say anything as he was so glad to get away.

Later that day, a friend phoned June and said, 'Someone broke into the Priory, got drunk on the Communion wine, smashed the place up and smeared shit everywhere.'

'That's awful,' June said, 'Have they caught anyone?'

'No,' she said, 'they haven't, but we know who they were, they were seen.'

'Well, you should go straight to the Police,' June said hotly. 'Who was it?'

There was a moment's silence. 'It was your Terry.'

June gave a little gasp; it had all the hallmarks of Terry.

'It's true you know,' her friend said. 'I would stake my life on it.'

June was nodding, 'Yes, I'm afraid it sounds all too familiar, oh dear,' she sighed.

When David arrived home that night, he told us of the morning's events and there was absolutely no doubt in our minds. We tried to figure out the psychology of this. How could it be justified? Did he feel that Patrick had somehow edged him out?

'He might as well have shit in Patrick's coffin,' I said, 'How the hell are we going to face Father Ronaldo? He won't want to do Patrick's service, will he? If I were him, I'd tell us all to sod off!'

There were reports of burglaries at several houses in the streets behind us. TV's and videos had been stolen. It couldn't have come at a worse time and the whole thing made me sick.

'You have to go and report it to the Police,' June said to David.

'They'll think I was in on it,' he protested.

'No they won't! Just tell them exactly what happened, you have nothing to fear!'

He reluctantly agreed and a day or so later, he met Terry in the town and told him he'd been to the Police to report the incident.

Terry retorted, 'Who gives a shit?'

'We know it was you who shit all over the priory, you might just as well have gone and shit in Patrick's coffin.'

Terry denied it and swore it wasn't him.

Patrick's natural parents and some of their relations came from Ireland for the funeral and they were really lovely people, when we considered Molly, his natural mother. Although we were very fond of her, she was a really needy girl and an alcoholic, in stark contrast to her wonderful family, I found that difficult to comprehend.

The boys bore the coffin into the Chapel. June and I, along with the rest of the family followed. The Priests and our Minister performed the ceremony as we'd hoped. So now it was the cemetery, this was it...the end.

Molly had specifically asked that he would be buried, not cremated and we promised her if he died, he would be. Later on, we had a little get together and Father Ronaldo was his usual self. I told him how sorry I was to hear about the incident of the break in.

He smiled and said, 'We have many bridges to cross in this life and I have already crossed that one.'

I shook my head in disbelief, 'Well, I have to say, you're a better man than I am, because I don't think I could take it like that.'

He smiled again and patting my arm he said, 'I'm sure it wouldn't trouble you at all.'

Robbie.

A few weeks elapsed, then we were contacted and asked if we would take Robbie who was half-Thai, just two years old and had Down syndrome. All my old fears came up again, I immediately thought of Megan and how nothing had ever been resolved, but we decided to go ahead.

'It won't hurt us to foster this little one,' June said.

We knew that he would never take the place of Patrick, and that wasn't the reason for taking him in any case. He was very tiny, not quite the size of a one-year-old and only just able to stand. He kept trying to balance but invariably tottered and went down with a bump on his backside; there was nothing wrong with his muscle tone. He learned to put his head on the floor, stick his backside in the air and run in circles round his head which stayed in the same spot; it was highly amusing. This was a very busy time for us as we got embroiled in taking him to therapy, clinic, music therapy and access. He was a beautiful child and didn't really look Down syndrome. His very black hair grew rapidly and everyone said, 'Isn't she beautiful?'

Having been a hairdresser, June decided to trim it up; it was the nearest thing to a war. He screamed, blubbered, tore at his tormentor and finally had to be held while she did a little bit of snipping.

The access with his parents and two older sisters revealed why he was so tiny; the whole family was tiny. His mother was extremely volatile and during the visits attacked the staff, and his social worker. I was spared all of this as June was taxied to and from the access.

'What do you think of Robbie's haircut?' June asked.

'I don't know, it looks a bit... I suppose it's all right, why, did you cut it again?'

She shook her head. 'No, I didn't, his mum did; I was horrified, she plonked him on her knee and fished a pair of wallpapering scissors out of her bag, then whacked off great big clumps of hair.'

'I bet he yelled his head off,' I said.

'No, that's the funny thing, he didn't. He sat bolt upright and never uttered a sound. I wasn't going to interfere because she's really unstable and the scissors were about twelve inches long. She was very frightening, and later on she went crazy at the social worker; she chased her down the stairs and threw tables and chairs after her, luckily, she escaped without injury.'

We became very attached to Robbie and knowing the problems of trans-racial placements, we had our doubts when we applied for his adoption, especially with the way Billy's adoption had gone awry because of the culture thing. When I think about this, I feel quite frustrated, because, take Billy for example, his Southern Irish Catholic half was also totally ignored, as if obliterated.

Almost immediately Social Workers arrived with Thai leaflets and documentation on Buddhism to assist in 'keeping Robbie's culture on track.' His English half was also totally disregarded. All the emphasis was on his 'black' identity.

We took it upon ourselves to ensure that the culture of all the children in our care was respected and kept alive, whether it was Buddhism, Catholicism, Muslim, or whatever; because we at least felt it was important.

Robbie's adoption was heard in the High Court and they were very quick to tell us, 'It's the highest Court in the land!' We found that a rather daunting prospect, however, the Judge said he thought we had done an excellent job and our family was the best place for him and sanctioned the adoption. We agreed to keep contact with his natural parents and his sisters. During the time we fostered Robbie leading up to his adoption, we also took his sisters on numerous holidays with us and also other frequent occasions, to give respite to their short-term carers during holiday breaks, outings and so forth.

Social Services started looking for a permanent placement for the girls and we said that we would be happy to foster them long term. The verdict of the 'team' was: 'it would not be in Robbie's best interest to place the girls with us, as it could jeopardise his placement.'

We scratched our heads in wonder at this, they had never jeopardised him during the numerous periods we'd had them previously; everything went off without a hitch every time. Anyway, the powers that be in their infinite wisdom, placed them for adoption, but they were later removed, being the victims of terrible abuse. They were then placed in other consecutive foster placements, all of which, broke down, causing one move after another and finally culminating in them being separated. During all of these goings on, we kept in contact with them and visited them on birthday's, Christmas and the like. Approximately eight years elapsed, then the powers that be came up with a wonderful idea? We should have them! We thought that was very 'original.' Unfortunately, we had in the interim period moved on and were no longer in a position to take them as we had other commitments. We found it really sad and thought that they had been irretrievably damaged by mishandling from the outset. Even so, we still carried on seeing them and had them on visits. It was so distressing to see how the chopping and changing in the 'system' left its indelible mark. However, I note that one of these girls recently celebrated the birth of her child and I was delighted at the news.

During the early days of having Robbie, we took part in a television program that went out on national television, I was rather pleased about that, it gave us some sort of recognition for our sustained efforts.

Moving on.

Finally, a date was set for Annie to be moved on and June said her room would have to be cleaned up. She quite got the hump about that, but June said: 'Don't worry! I'll give you a hand with that!'

'Oh, that would be nice,' she twittered.

June said to Billy, 'You can have Annie's room when she goes, you would like that, wouldn't you?'

He screwed his face up in horror and I knew immediately what his concerns were, so I raised my hands and said, 'It's alright, you can help me scrub it out and redecorate it so that it'll be like a new room. We'll get you all new furniture and bedding; is that okay?' He accepted that.

While helping her to clear up, among the debris, June came across around six pairs of her own knickers, with the crutch cut out of them; she wondered where they had gone. Annie was going around the room, singing happily: 'La, la la, la la, la' she went as she pulled the curtains back and smiled as she said: 'Shall I wash these up?'

June did a double take and instantly knew why the children kept saying that her room smelt so bad. On the window sill were our six, best cut-glass, quite expensive wine glasses, full of shit! As though it was perfectly normal, June said, 'Yes, I think that would be best.'

When she told me, I was so shocked and said, 'So that's what the awful smell was; yuk!' You are going to dump them, aren't you?'

'Absolutely!' She said, screwing her face up.

When the room was cleared, there was still the strong smell of shit. Billy and I went in with the cleaning gear and started scrubbing it, top to bottom, even the ceiling. We cleared it completely and burnt all the furniture, bedding, curtains and the carpet. I knew that I needed to obliterate all traces of her to assure him.

Billy said, 'There's something smelly behind this radiator.'

I said, 'go and fetch my big long screwdriver.'

Peering down at it, I started to fish it out and as it came into view, Billy, who was holding a black bag open, started screaming and running on the spot. It was a type of long woollen stocking and around nine inches of the foot end was plastered in shit. I slapped it into the bag, knotted it and put it on the fire straight away. Then took the radiator off, stripped the wall-paper, scrubbed behind it and painted everything to satisfy him that the place was clean.

Never having heard how the majority of previous foster children fared after they moved on, it was a bit of a surprise when we were asked if we would visit Annie. She was in a special secure unit, a sort of bridging placement until they sorted out a permanent place. A week or so after she left, we received the terrible news that she had been gang raped in an underpass; so much for safe keeping!

We went to see her in the secure unit. It had a highly intensive security system with special locks. I thought they were crackers with all the wonderful security, as the children were let out in the mornings to wander the streets willy-nilly during the day and into the evening; unsupervised. That was how she ended up the victim of the so-called gang rape. I found the whole thing utterly ridiculous and said to June, 'So much for another place of safety!'

Shortly afterwards, she was moved to another place that was renowned for its wonderful work with this sort of child, and they were quite insistent that we should visit her to continue the link. I was amazed at the marvellous surroundings, the grandeur of the buildings; the setting was absolutely idyllic. Annie had grown a lot and by this time looked quite chubby. We were given a grand welcome and offered some refreshments. She was eager to show us around and walked ahead of us while her Support Worker, a thirty-something woman walked with us and told us how marvellously she was doing. Annie announced proudly as her worker let us in with her huge bunch of keys: 'This is my bedroom.'

It was a dormitory, housing I suppose in the region of twenty. Each bed was sectioned off with little cupboards and her section was surprisingly neat and tidy. I wondered just how anyone would be able to 'Police' the sleeping quarters.

'We're not allowed in here during the day, it's out of bounds,' she said and smiled, then giving her worker a coy look, she pointed, 'But we leave that window open and get in anyway, don't we?'

Her worker gave a half shrug and smiled knowingly. During the course of the meeting, she kept giving her worker big hugs and was generally very familiar with her.

'Come to the kitchen and we'll get you some coffee!' Annie said.

Her worker didn't object and went quite happily along with her directions. Once again, we had to be let in through each door as they were all locked.

'Hello Charlie!' Annie called loudly in a very familiar way to a man working in the kitchen. As we walked through to the seating area, she grabbed a large banana off a fruit bowl. 'I think I'll have a banana,' she said then peeled it and took a huge bite. I wondered what her worker's reactions would be but she didn't object. We had coffee and her worker suggested that Annie should show us round the rest of the school, and as we proceeded, I thought all the pupils had to be on their break. There were two teachers smoking cigarettes in the first classroom, both had their feet up on a work bench. I was quite surprised that smoking was permitted in the classroom. We went from class to class and it was the same scenario; finally, we came to the pottery class. There were no students in any of the classrooms and these teachers were also sitting smoking, and one had his feet up on the workbench. The pottery class quite fascinated me, I was very keen on pottery having done courses on it, and had a kiln of my own that I used regularly. Their equipment was state of the art, far superior to mine, capable of even doing porcelain, so I asked to see some of the work that was being done. I was astonished that there were no finished projects, or even one's in progress that I could have a look at.

'When does the class resume?' I asked, quite eager to see how they went about things.

'Oh, it won't be resuming, there isn't anyone in class today, you see they don't have to come in if they don't want to, that's the rule here.'

Was I hearing things? I realised immediately why all the classes were empty. As we walked on, Annie pointed through a window to a clear view of the woods and we could see a number of young teenagers, (playing?) unsupervised.

'That's where we go and play,' she said. 'Sometimes we play up there.' She pointed to a flat roof. 'We just hop up here,' she tapped brickwork that jutted out, 'And run along that wall and play there; all day sometimes.'

When we left, I felt as though I had been dreaming. These (children) all young teenagers approaching or in some cases over sixteen.

'How much do they charge for keeping a child at this place?' I asked June.

'Between fifteen hundred and two thousand pounds a week each,' she replied.

At that time, we received, around ten per cent of that for children in our care. I was shocked and said, 'Excuse my French, but I think it's the biggest load of crap I've ever seen in my life.'

Later on, we got regular phone calls from Annie telling us that she had been to the cinema with some of the others. She was always very keen to let us know that the films were X rated, which of course were '18,' something we had never permitted. We had kept strict boundaries regarding age limits on film categories when she was with us, as we did with all the children. It seemed to me that they had no restrictions, rules, boundaries or any sort of guidance. The next thing we heard was that she ran away, was picked up by the Police, screamed abuse at them and kicked their car causing quite a lot of damage.

'I don't know,' I sighed, 'Just what sort of preparation for life are they giving these kids? They have a free hand to do exactly what they want, then everyone wonders why they run amok and end up having problems or even end up in prison when they have to fend for themselves.'

June said it was not her problem, it was out of her hands.

Someone tried several times to make a reverse charge phone call from Annie's area and as they were quite persistent, in the end, June accepted the call; just in case it was important.

'Is that Annie's Foster Mum?' A young girl, with a broad London accent asked. 'I fought you'd bett'r know, Annie went out joy riding wiv some fella's last night and they crashed the car and she was killed.'

June, stunned to silence, didn't reply but slowly put the phone down.

Staring through me she said, 'That was a friend of Annie's, she was out joy riding with some boys last night and was killed...'

'Good God!' I gasped, 'Is it true?'

'I don't think so,' she said. 'I'm going to phone back and find out.'

A social worker answered: 'oh, hello Misses Crowe, yes, Annie's here and she's very upset; she didn't know her friend was making that call to you.'

'Can I speak to her?' June asked.

Annie, ostensibly very distressed, was blubbering on the other end and June snapped, 'Come off it Annie! Do you think I'm stupid? It had to be your idea, how else would she have got my number?'

Her friend, who had to be listening in, burst out laughing along with her, and when Annie managed to control her outburst, she said, 'It was just a little April fool joke, after all, it is the first of April.'

June said, 'perhaps you thought it was funny, I didn't.'

When she told me, I said, 'Why do we put up with this nonsense?'

We had put a lot into visiting and generally running around since she had left us, there was never any financial assistance despite the fact it cost us dearly each time we went; she was 'out of care' as far as we were concerned. The round trip was getting on for two hundred miles and they drafted a timetable that we had to adhere to each time we were asked to visit; correction, told to visit! That actually got up my nose, especially as they were getting around a couple of thousand pounds a week for doing what I saw as sod all.

She was moved to a flat of her own, and told us that she had four permanent workers on a rota, covering her twenty-four hours a day.

Quite a few months later, we received a call from her and she was really excited. 'I'm doing my NVQ in childcare, and I travel to a nursery every day where I look after children; isn't that good?'

June asked her who had arranged all of this.

'Social services arranged everything, so what do you think of that?'

When June told me, I was more than flabbergasted. 'What idiot has dreamt up this impending disaster?' I gasped, 'We can't let this happen, I have to do something about it!'

I wrote a letter to the agency saying that Annie had four permanent workers on a rota covering her twenty-four hours a day, but is doing an NVQ level 3 in child care and travels to work in a Nursery every day. What would the unsuspecting parents of these children think and do if they knew just what was going on? I can only thank God that my children, or grandchildren are not attending this nursery. I had to say that I didn't blame Annie at all, but rather the misguided idiot who has arranged it. Do you think you would be able to do something about this before it is too late? Later, we were informed that her training in that particular sphere was suspended and I breathed a sigh of relief.

Task-centred work.

We moved on, into what was known as 'task-centred work,' which meant we took children with problems that could be classed as serious. In the same category as Norman, Terry, Don and Annie I suppose; personally, I couldn't see the difference.

'Surely they don't come any worse than them?' I said, but to quote my kids, 'I was having a laugh,' of course they do!

We were placed Thomas, a ten-year-old boy and within a few weeks, our kids said they didn't like him much at all; even I thought he was a bit odd. After some negotiations, June managed to get him into the local school, but getting him into school was just the beginning, we had to buy school equipment, then there was his school uniform and last of all his school dinners. Back then, things always seemed a bit hectic on Monday mornings.

'He needs money for school dinners,' June said.

I rifled through my pockets. 'I haven't got any change; I'll have to give him this,' I said holding a ten-pound note up. I looked at her questioningly and she shrugged.

'Here you are then; you'll have to bring the change back! Okay?'

He shrugged as I gave it to him, and his attitude made me feel a bit uncomfortable. Later on, the school phoned and said he hadn't turned up, and much later on his Social Worker phoned and informed us that he had been picked up by the Police, 'would I go and fetch him as there is no one else to do it?'

After some persuasion and pressurising, I reluctantly agreed. Quite honestly, I didn't relish the thought of the hundred-and-sixty-miles' journey both ways, not to mention picking up this peculiar boy on my own. I felt alone, exposed and vulnerable, knowing all too well how Social Workers react when there is an allegation. The closer I got, the more I felt like a sitting duck.

Building alterations were being carried out at the Police Station, and at the front, they had a Portakabin serving as a make-shift office. The Police sergeant, smiled and said; 'There'll be someone along shortly to take you to where he is being held.'

A constable arrived and as we walked round the back towards a separate block, there was a hell of a racket coming from it as we approached. I did a double take and the constable smiled. He gave a little nod towards the noise, 'Busy night tonight, we've had a load of drunks in.'

I gave a little mirthless laugh, 'Well it does sound a bit... well...'

He chuckled. 'Yes! I know what you mean.'

He unlocked the outer door and then locked it behind me, and I was ushered into a small cell like office. There was screaming, whooping and lots of very loud banging of a heavy metal door being constantly kicked by several people; the noise was horrendous. During the din, there was a continuous stream of uniformed Police Officers into the office, giving details of different prisoners. I waited while all this was going on until the Sergeant asked me for the boy's details. I hadn't a clue, we had known him a very short time, so I had to phone home and get them from June.

'Right then,' the sergeant said with an air of authority, 'Let's go and fetch him! I think he'll be pleased to see you; he's been banged up for eleven hours.'

I nodded in agreement, 'I suppose he will,' I muttered.

We approached the door that was being kicked, the racket, along with the shouting was almost ear splitting. Several people were screaming a song so loud that it was distorted and completely out of tune. When he clanked the key in the cell door, the racket stopped as though switched off. It was not unlike a twenty-foot container, completely devoid of any furnishings, there were over a dozen young boys, ranging from around ten to the eldest about fourteen, standing glowering. Thomas was right at the front and looked as though he'd been dragged through a hedge backwards, his new school uniform was completely ruined.

'Green? Which one is Thomas Green?' The sergeant called, looking around the group.

Thomas screwed his face into a scowl, 'Not me! Never heard of him!'
He snarled.

I pointed my finger and said, 'That's him!'

The Sergeant jerked his thumb over his shoulder twice. 'Right mister, out! C'mon! Your Foster father has come to take you home!'

He stuffed his hands deep into his pockets, and swinging bodily from one foot to the other, he strutted slowly and belligerently towards us. He stopped and looked up, scowling into my face, 'I'm not getting in the car!' He hissed. 'I know this area really well, and if you force me to go, I will run away the minute you stop!'

'I think I had better phone Social Services,' I said to the Sergeant.

'Right then, come with me,' he said and we went back to the cell like office.

I said, 'I'll have to phone my missus to get the 'out-of-hours' number.'

Thomas rattled off a number.

'What?' I said.

'Go on!' He said, 'That's the number! Ring that number and they will ask who you are, where you are, and they'll tell you to hang up, then an Out-of-Hours Social Worker will call you back.'

I wondered just how many times this little sod had done this. I rang the number he gave me and it went exactly as he had predicted.

The sergeant said, 'While you are waiting for the call from the Social Services, would you mind coming with me?'

He ushered us into another container like cell, with a couple of chairs in. I was shocked when he locked the door behind us. I felt vulnerable, and extremely uncomfortable. I wouldn't put it past this boy to bash his own head against the wall, then lie on the floor and scream abuse. The worst part of that would be, they would actually believe him, and I could find myself in prison for child abuse! I was surprised and relieved when he stuffed his hands deep into his pockets again and shuffled an imaginary particle of dust around with his foot; I took a seat.

'Where's your tie?'

'Threw it away!' He snapped.

'Where's my ten pounds?'

'Gone!'

'Is this what you want out of life? To spend your youth banged up in Police cells and maybe even prison?' I asked.

'I've had a great time with my mates; we've had a good laugh,' he said.

There was no point in talking to this kid, so we stayed there in silence until they took him back to the cells and fetched me to answer the phone; it was June.

'He is refusing to get in the car and I am certainly not going to force him. His school uniform is knackered and his tie is gone, so is my tenner and all of his school equipment.'

'Ah well, never mind,' she said, 'just tell the Social worker he refuses to go with you and they'll have to make other arrangements; book into a hotel for the night if you want!'

Life was a bit of a struggle since I'd had the operation and she was worried that the drive would be too much. Even though it was after twelve thirty by the time I finished talking to the Social Worker, I decided to make the journey back.

About six weeks or so later, we were asked if we would take a ten-year-old boy for a few weeks.

'These ten-year old's, they get more plentiful by the minute,' I chuckled.

When they said his name was Thomas Green, I thought I was hearing things.

'I wouldn't touch him with a barge pole.' I said.

He, like so many others, was the type of kid who had learned how to abuse the system and didn't care who he injured in the process. 'Thanks, but no thanks!'

June told them that we were unable to take anyone at the moment.

I said to June, 'I think there should be a file made up on this type of child and available to foster parents. It could be accessed, then they wouldn't be able to dump them on unsuspecting families. That would leave precious resources available for children who really are in need and can use what a family like ours has to offer.'

She looked sideways at me, 'Huh! You wish!'

'Ah well, no harm in trying, is there?' I laughed.

Jenny.

Shortly afterwards, we took Jenny, a little three-year-old girl who by all accounts came from a very deprived background, and had a question mark over her; was she sexually abused? At this time, we hadn't got a spare room, so she would have to sleep in Patrick's cot in our room. I didn't like that idea much and decided to bunk down elsewhere; she was only with us briefly.

There were a few of us sitting in the living room watching television. She was sitting on the settee between June and Sammy and I was in the armchair. She was a right little chatterbox and suddenly, in the middle of her chattering, she said, 'Jerry puts his willie in my front wee-wee and my back wee-wee.' She held her hands out, with her index fingers about six inches apart, 'His willie is like that but it's not as big as Daddy's.'

Sammy cried, 'Mother, please tell me that my ears are not telling my brain what this child is saying!'

June was silent, wide eyed, her mouth open in shock. We reported it to Social Services but never heard anything more. Almost immediately, she was moved on; never to be heard of again.

William.

I'm not sure if the placing Authority knew what we were letting ourselves in for when we agreed to take William, but if they didn't, they found out in no time at all, as did we.

When they place a child, they are always subject to home visits. To say William was not the most intelligent child would be more than kind. He had red hair, with the look of Irish about him, twelve years old and big for his age. He came from a children's home and when we visited him, I thought he seemed okay. During our visits, he bragged continuously to the other children about his new family saying: 'I've got an 'orse,' referring to our little Shetland pony.

He was quite happy and eager to get the initial visits over and move in. On the day that John, his residential Social Worker brought him to finally settle in, he was extremely distressed and hung onto John howling, and asking him to take him back.

In an effort to comfort him John said, 'Sure if you don't like it here, you can always come back to us.'

I thought that was a very destructive bit of work on his part. If William had been a fire cracker, John could not have more effectively lit the fuse. We took William to McDonald's where I had a big talk with him, he seemed to understand very well and ended up crying on my shoulder.

'But I don't want to be here,' he sobbed. 'I want to be at my old school.'

Understanding all too well what was going on in his mind, I did my best to console him. My memories of 'The School' still haunt me. On the rare occasions that I pass by where it once stood, I still stop and have a wistful look, I suppose in an abortive hope to catch a glimpse of a ghost of the past; no one can console you in this situation.

'You just have to give yourself time,' I told him.

We weren't to know that 'time' to William was a nonentity. William made a calculated decision that he was going to return to his old school. 'His old school' was a part of every sentence he uttered and his utterances were many. Knowing that if he didn't like it with us, he could always go back again, fuelled his emotions and was instrumental in his outrageous behaviour. If it was outrageous enough, we would have no alternative but to have him removed; to his old school, of course, and they would once again have their considerable remuneration for looking after him, which I thought sparked off John's remark in the first place.

He shouted at June, 'Fuck off and leave me alone, you fucking old slag!'

Then he physically attacked her which was extremely worrying. His outbursts, after several hours of continual shouting and screaming, culminated with him taking his case and walking to the top of the hill in the freezing cold and rain. That lasted several hours, during which time he stood at the top end of the street, continuously screaming that we were a bunch of fucking bastards! On his exit, he also left the front door wide open and June went frantic. During all of this, William being so much the centre of attention, Robbie could not be found. She thought he must have ran out onto the road, but we found him cowering in a corner. He had totally withdrawn because of the awful racket.

June phoned out-of-hours and was told; 'Out of hours will not come out for a (tantrum?)' In the end, when he returned, still in his wet clothes, he had to be physically carried in and put on his bed. He calmed down a little that night, but his outrageous behaviour resumed the following morning, 22nd December. It was slightly different in that he did not physically attack June this time, just verbal abuse and spitting throughout the period until his social worker came to the house. She sat with him in the back room for a couple of hours and he expressed a lot of sadness at leaving his old school. She got him to agree to be calm so that we could do some Christmas shopping the next day. The fact that he had no notion of time was made clear. He had been with us a month and told us he had tried this for four days and didn't like it, so he wanted to go back to his old school. So, what is summer to William? Tomorrow? Next week? Who knows? Anyway, the result was, immediately upon Pat the social worker's departure, he ran amok for hours and had to be carried to his bedroom again. Later he materialised again and physically attacked June, spat on her then stormed out of the house and was returned to the house by the police. They came on the misconception that a child was being abused. When we informed Social Services, Pat said that she would come on Wednesday. Neither June nor I felt that this was in the best interest of his stability, which was very fragile in any case. However, much to our dismay, Pat was adamant, but the meeting didn't materialise, she didn't even turn up in any case. Some time later, the really efficient charity, that had placed Paul, was enlisted in an attempt to get the placement to work.

Christmas, being a very busy time in our household, seemed to hold him in abeyance and we had a calm spell. On the 20th January, he really went berserk, while we had a Social Worker visiting us about Robbie's welfare, bringing with her, more leaflets on Buddhism to ensure his half-Thai culture continued. At the same time, our Insurance Man turned up to discuss a policy. William was very calculating and picked his time when he knew the effect would be most devastating. After several hours of frenzied behaviour, we managed to get him to his bedroom. Shortly afterwards I could hear crashing and banging going on upstairs. June was fearful that I would be unable to cope with what was taking place. She begged me to stay away and not confront him. She tends to forget that I have seen and experienced more violence and mayhem than even William could produce. The extremely tough Children's Home that I was in ensured that and prior to that, I lived in one of the toughest areas of Belfast City.

She was under immense stress; her lips were white and I was fearful for her welfare. Even so, I went to see just what devastation he had wreaked. I was shocked and certain that no one would believe what had taken place, so I got my camera to photograph it. When he saw me trying to photograph it, he pelted me with every item he could lay his hands on, and to add insult to injury, the flash on the camera wouldn't work, so I was unable to photograph it in any case. His little escapade caused hundreds of pounds' worth of damage. We took our Insurance Man up to have a look. He said the damage was between six and seven hundred pounds. He laughed when we asked about a claim and he said, 'But this isn't accidental damage; is it?' I had to agree.

William had had no food at all that day, as this episode started when he was asked to wash when he was getting up in the morning. Meals were made for him but he was determined that he would carry his project through. At about four o'clock, when the Insurance man left, he erupted with a renewed zeal, and attacked June. He had to be physically held down on the floor by June, our son Peter, and his friend Allan. This carried on for over an hour while he screamed and went into a frenzy, head butting June twice, kicking and spitting at everyone including me. He was scarlet and looked as though he was in danger of passing out with rage. When he finally calmed down, he sat on June's lap, sucking his thumb and behaving like an infant. We had another period of relative calm and I would say that this was due to the fact that June neither asked him to do, or not do anything.

We had to buy him a complete set of new clothes because the ones he came in were utterly useless, being size nine to ten. He was a thirty-four chest and had long since outgrown every single item. He couldn't even get his wellies or his shoes on as they were all too small apart from the ones he came in.

On the 20th of January, a few days before June's birthday, I took him in the car to the shops to get a card for her and he wanted to get one as well. When we got back, a friend had popped by in his lorry for a visit and William wanted to help around the lorry. June said if he was going to do anything like that, would he please take his new clothes off and wear something 'old.'

He flew into a rage and screamed that she was a fucking old slag, and she needn't think he was going to take his new boots or coat off, because he wasn't! Once again, he turned violent and with great difficulty we managed to get him to his bedroom. June told him if he felt angry, he could be angry in his bedroom and not let it spill out over the rest of the house. Talking to him infuriated him even more, and his behaviour enraged our children. When June came down the stairs, she looked quite ill and said: 'I've just taken an awful kicking from that little sod and he's broken my glasses.'

He had punched and kicked her and then attempted to throttle her. To say that I was furious was an understatement. I went to his bedroom and found Sammy holding the door. William was on the inside, yanking at the handle, screaming and kicking, trying to open it. I jerked my thumb sideways at Sammy and said, 'go!' When he moved aside, I burst into his room and shouted, 'Sit!' And pointed at the bed. He must have thought I meant business because he obeyed without hesitation. I told him his behaviour disgusted me, especially as it was June's birthday tomorrow. I said that I certainly would not tolerate him attacking me. I think I was pretty convincing because he calmed right down, and I had quite a long talk with him. Once again, he sobbed on my shoulder, saying that he didn't want to be here.

In the meantime, the Police arrived expecting to have to take him into protective custody. They were astonished at the mess and the damage but when they saw that I had the situation under control, they were reluctant to interfere. They did give him a talking to and said if he behaved himself, he would be invited to the Police Station to have a look around and see the horses. I thought that was a bit stupid, rewarding this little monster for acting like a maniac; goodness knows what their logic was. Anyway, he was quite excited about that and said that he thought the Police were really nice. He then said that he thought he would be a policeman when he grew up, but I told him that it would be very unlikely that he would ever be considered for the Police Force as it would now be very well documented that he is a violent person. This was their third visit inside a month, how would that look if he was to apply?

In the days that followed, he reverted to his usual twittering, as though nothing had happened and we had a period of relative calm. Unfortunately, he had another one of his violent outbursts during which he left the front door open and Robbie managed to get out. We had always been very strict on exit doors for that reason. Everyone except William ran frantically searching for Robbie but to no avail; he was gone! June phoned the police and they said they'd had a report that an old lady had taken a small boy into her flat. June went to see if it was Robbie and it was. The old lady was very reluctant to hand him over and said, 'He could have been killed on the road, you know.'

When June arrived home, she said she was so relieved and grateful to the old lady that she would take her a bunch of flowers tomorrow. When she arrived with the flowers, the old lady was very confused and couldn't understand what the flowers were for.

'For looking after my little boy,' June said.

'What? I haven't got your little boy!'

'I know that! It's for yesterday, you remember, my little boy?'

'I don't know your little boy and I certainly haven't got him,' she replied.

When June returned home, she said, 'she couldn't even remember the incident.'

I said, 'Well at least he's safe now, isn't he?'

On Saturday, June had to go to Slough for a 'Charity' advertising campaign. So, I had William for the day and even at this stage, I was still surprised at his intelligence level, his topics of conversation and his general communication. He said that he used to love the police coming to his house; they came all the time and it was absolutely brilliant; a real treat because he loved their blue flashing lights.

Needless to say, we couldn't carry on with the placement, it was a bit like having a rabid dog for a pet and expecting not to be bitten, so he returned to his old school and they presumably took over where we left off.

Despite the fact that his authority gave us a copy of their wonderful special insurance, covering us in the event of any damage relating to William, or his placement. When we asked repeatedly for compensation for the damage he caused, which when June's new glasses costing one hundred and fifty pounds were added, tallied up to around nine hundred pounds, all their assurances evaporated. Not only did they renege on that, they never even paid for his new clothes that were absolutely essential. We made repeated applications for those and numerous other expenses incurred during the introduction. A couple of cheques came which gave us a little towards our expenses but this was quickly followed by four different written demands that we return them. June said we would have to send them back, but I said we most certainly would not! I wrote back each time saying that we still hadn't been reimbursed for the damage or expenses. That was ignored; we got nothing! We came away with it costing us well over five hundred pounds and I couldn't help thinking that at the price, we'd actually had a very lucky escape from a greedy, mercenary, parsimonious, lying, cheating authority that wanted as much as possible for as little as possible, or should I say, something for nothing!

In those days, some authorities were very slow in meeting payments, so it was easy for them to withhold payments later. I said in my letter to them, that if the roles were reversed, we would very quickly end up in court and the fact that we didn't, speaks volumes. Unfortunately, this was not an isolated case.

George.

With William gone, we had a space that could be filled and we were placed George. On the face of it, George came over as a lovely ten-year-old. He was of good appearance, well-spoken and appeared to be very well mannered; that sounds good, doesn't it? Unfortunately, underneath all that lay a very devious, quite cruel child who required undivided attention at all times. We took him and Robbie, who by this time was three years old, on holiday to a country cottage in Wales. June was horrified when she caught him red handed trying to push Robbie, into the open log fire. As she entered the room, she screamed, 'ah!' Which fortunately stopped him in his tracks, what a piece of luck she came upon him when she did! We had several other incidents but nothing quite so drastic. His allocated social worker said that he was a lovely boy and wondered if we were having an adverse effect on him. The Lady Therapist, who had been attending Annie, was called upon to see what she thought about his behaviour. We later found out that the fire thing wasn't an isolated incident. In a previous foster situation, another child luckily escaped serious injury when he pushed her down a flight of stairs. We felt we should press on in any case, it just meant we would have to be ever more vigilant.

They told us, 'You shouldn't confront him! Oh no! That could be very damaging!' The hair brained ideas that we were bound by, left us no way of controlling or admonishing him and he was very quick to spot that, and made our lives a misery.

I wondered how people who sometimes have no experience of raising children and in some cases have none of their own, end up making decisions that carers have to abide by, often to the detriment of the child.

A review was set up and we were amazed to find it was a disruption meeting, to end the placement. We were totally excluded while all the decisions were made. The whole thing was so amateurish and incompetent, as were all the dealings; including the remuneration! I considered the events that took place and found it so depressing; it made me angry! Any prospects of success had been trashed. I felt so sorry for June, all her best efforts had been to no avail and of course there was George, what chance did he have? He would in all probability be put in a children's home, which can be devastating. In all our years of fostering, we had never heard of a review taking place when the actual foster carers were excluded. We thought it was crazy, but there was nothing we could do about it. I decided that the least I could do, would be to let them know just how I felt in a letter that went something like:

Re: Events at meeting on 22nd March.

Since the removal on the 22nd of our parenting role when we were unable to contribute to the review. We didn't even know what our task was until after the meeting. The cart has been put before the horse! With the present financial arrangements, I feel that this will be damaging to us and him. We were, and still are, very shocked at how low the allowances were but proceeded in an abortive attempt to make do.

Taking a child like George and attempting to manage on a shoe string, does not benefit us and certainly does not benefit the child, it can only lead to hardship for all concerned.

George was removed and went to a children's home. So, the authority's bill would have multiplied perhaps ten-fold, and he would not have the benefit of a 'family life.' I am sure that when he reaches eighteen, he would then be 'dumped' on an unsuspecting public as was the case with so many of these kids.

The fact that we lived in an ex-children's home, actually put us in virtually the same category expense wise as a children's home. Why did they expect us to manage extremely difficult tasks on pittance and to have part of the allowance classed as 'reward?' It would be laughable if it wasn't so pitiful, but in the end, it was the children who suffered. Nowadays, they are becoming more realistic and they don't quite so much try to hold you to ransom with emotional blackmail, using your dedication as a weapon against you. I have to say that back then, that was just how we found it and the sad thing was, so many children fell by the wayside because of it and then had money poured at them in torrents, to no avail. The end result was that we wound up at logger heads with our authority and subsequently resigned in disgust. This resignation was an extremely harrowing ordeal, dragged out over months.

A social worker friend said: 'Ask to see your records! They can write anything they like in them you know, and by law, they have to let you see them!'

We wrote several times asking to see them and also asked our social worker a number of times to arrange this. I became very angry when meetings were arranged with the head of Social Services; each time we made the two hour's journey each way, we were told to sit and wait for long periods in the office. Then someone came along each time and said, 'I'm afraid he won't be able to see you today; an emergency has cropped up.' After the third visit, it did an excellent job of making sure we didn't bother to arrange any further meetings. We phoned the office on other occasions and asked, but to this day, we have never seen our records.

At the outset, this was a wonderful authority, and we took pride in being a part of it, but over the years it became entrenched in left wing politics, political correctness and sometimes militant black or completely useless social workers who, either went over the top on grounds of ethnic background, or did absolutely nothing, as was the case with Alice and her allegation.

Over three years later out of the blue I received a letter that said: 'There were no grounds for the allegation that Alice made against me.' I was completely exonerated. That did wonders for me I must say, especially when they said as they left the meeting: 'there will be no secrets, we shall be back in touch within forty-eight hours.' What nonsense! We had moved on and had gone lecturing for different authorities to large classes of foster carers on: 'How to deal with an allegation.' What would be the worst scenario? Ours was thought to be just that, the only one that we thought outstripped ours, was our friend who hung himself.

The classes consisted of women. Invariably, I was the only man present, or perhaps, there would be a male social worker. I told them that I thought the men should be alerted to this sort of thing because the large percentage of allegations made, were against men, or the males in the household. That was the very reason that we supported families in trauma on a country wide basis, we had been there, came through it and survived, unlike the cases in America and here.

The Girls.

Off we went again, this time it was two Southern Irish Catholic siblings, eight and ten. I think that although they were terribly abused, this was an extremely rewarding venture, marred once again by incompetent and inept social workers.

What set these two young girls apart from most fostering situations was, they had very supportive grandparents who wanted to work with us. Instead of the usual scenario, where we were invariably seen as arch enemies by the birth family, who usually did their utmost to poison the child's mind against us, because they seemed to think we had colluded with the authorities in having their children removed in the first place, but not this time. We built a rapport with them and the girls. Sadly, the mother indulged in drinking binges with friends; we never really got to know her.

First off, along with another foster family, we took them on holiday and as we walked through a fun park, I felt uncomfortable how the eldest girl kept hanging onto my arm and generally being over attentive. A little while later when the girls were on the swings, I joined June and Carol and was about to say that I thought these children were very possibly sexually abused, when June said: 'Carol and I both think that these children are very possibly sexually abused.'

I said: 'That's what I was about to say.'

It's strange how alert one becomes after fostering sexually abused children. Some years ago, my son Peter said, 'I saw Julie; you remember Julie? I haven't seen her since we were children. I never knew she was sexually abused.'

'Good grief!' I said, 'Did she tell you that?'

'No, no, of course not! I just know.'

I nodded and thought, 'Yes, you do, don't you?'

Later on, when June was on her own with Nora, the older girl, she said: 'I am very old and very wise and I know when a child has been hurt in an inappropriate way.'

With that, Nora broke down and it all came spilling out. How her mother on occasions had friends' round and when they were all the worse for drink, one or other of the men would come to their bed in the night; her mother's boyfriends and even her friend's boyfriends. I thought that perhaps the perpetrators felt safe in the knowledge that the others would not wake up as they were all invariably the worse for drink. On one occasion, Nora decided to tell her mother what was going on and her mother flew into a rage and said: 'If you don't stop telling horrible lies, I will punish you severely.' Consequently, she never said anything again and the abuse continued until they were taken into care.

When they were first with us, I treated them with the utmost caution. I thought that I was on very thin ice with them, and that meant setting up strict boundaries for them and me. I adhered to these boundaries at all times. We told them that this was not only designed to keep them safe but ensured the safety of others; especially me. I was at no time left alone with them either together, or on their own. That way, there could never be an allegation false or otherwise that could go unchallenged. However, as time went by, we warmed to them so much that I was even able to give them little cuddles in the evenings, provided it was in the family setting with others present. I never dreamt that would be possible and prior to having them, it was completely out of the question. I found caring for them very rewarding and we grew to love them as though they were our own children. They finally left us and did very well. On the day they were leaving, their grandparents came and Nora flung her arms around me and said, 'I love you.'

I felt so proud to have been instrumental in hopefully giving these children back their childhood. I looked at their grandmother; she was smiling. I gave Nora a peck on the cheek and said, 'Me too sweetheart, I love you!'

It was so different to the breakdowns, removals, or just plain walkouts that we had become so accustomed to.

So, we moved on. Our new authority was so different, we had no problem warming to them and building a relationship that blossomed and carried on for many years, but alas, I fear that shades of what went on with our old authority crept in.

Asylum Seekers.

Almost by accident, we stepped into fostering young asylum seekers. This was a new and very different category to mainstream fostering. Initially, we hadn't a clue and by the same token, neither had our social workers, but as we were hands on, we very quickly learned. Our social workers blundered on in the dark, sometimes making the most idiotic decisions, especially if they were new to this particular branch of fostering. We were quite successful at this and have a number of these children who are very close to the family and still come to visit us, even after some twenty years. They were very secretive as to who sent them, how they arrived, where their family was, if they had a family. Did they have a family, was their family still alive? The main problem of course being, if they say there is a family back home, there was the risk they would then be repatriated, so invariably, they don't have a family and are granted leave to stay. The majority of them think that London is the 'Mother Lode,' the 'El Dorado,' this mythical goldmine is the stuff of dreams. Initially they will stop at nothing to get there and it doesn't matter if they make your life a misery in the process. If, given time, they do actually settle down, then having them can be very rewarding. Quite a contrast to mainstream fostering. The main difference with asylum seeker children, once they have settled, is that they actually want to be in a family and very soon became imbedded in ours.

Misguided social workers do tend to make a difficult task virtually impossible. We were placed a fifteen-year-old boy from somewhere on the continent, and he spoke reasonably good English. He said that he didn't want to be here, he wanted to be with his uncle who lived over a hundred miles away. By law, social services have to have a place Police checked before they allow a child to move in, so his uncle had to be checked. This process can take many weeks or even months and who did he blame? Us, of course! As he was a Muslim, we felt that our first task should be to take him to the Mosque. The nearest one was quite a jaunt and because it was only open on Fridays and being Friday, as usual the traffic was awful. Fortunately, we left very early, but because of road works and long delays, after a two-hour journey, we managed to get him there half an hour before it started. It lasted just over an hour and then we waited for around three quarters of an hour after it was over while he mixed with other men who spoke his language. By the time we arrived home, the episode had taken over five hours. I was quite surprised and more than a little pleased when he said he didn't like it, and didn't want to go again.

He smoked like a chimney and I said that it was illegal for me to buy him cigarettes. When I refused, he went snooping around our other, older foster boy's room and stole them; the boy was furious!

Shortly after he arrived, we took him to a restaurant some seven miles away and he was delighted. They spoke his language and he conversed with them the whole time we were there. It cost us over twenty pounds, but we were pleased that he had enjoyed it, so we took him to another one, three miles away. Upon a second visit to the first restaurant, the lady serving us, who spoke impeccable English, made a point of coming to our table and quite aggressively, told us how horrible we were for not letting him go to stay with his uncle. Because of that, we really didn't like the idea of going back there.

He wanted to phone his family and we did allow him to do so on several occasions; at our expense. Social Services arranged a review and along came, what we later classed as (a new breed) of social worker, who almost immediately made me bristle as she wielded her authority like a Prima-Donna.

'Oh, that's nice,' she said, 'They took you to a nice restaurant; you liked that, didn't you?'

He smiled. 'Yes!'

'And you liked the other one as well, didn't you?'

Smiling, he nodded again, 'Yes!'

'Very well. Jim will take you to the first restaurant three times a week and he will also take you three times a week to the other one! I gawked in disbelief and June mutely signalled me to be silent.

'You're a Muslim, aren't you?' She continued.

'Yes.'

'Of course, you would like to go to the Mosque! Wouldn't you?'

He paused for a while, pondering and then said, 'er, yes.'

'Okay!' She said smiling. 'Jim will take you to the Mosque every Friday!' When I objected, our social worker shook her head telling me to shut up.

'You like to phone your family, don't you?' She continued.

He smiled broadly.

'Jim will get you a five-pound phone card every week so that you can phone home!' She glanced at June and said abruptly: 'And you can monitor his phone calls!'

That was a joke as during his calls, he spoke his own language. The phone card was a disaster, it turned out to be a penny a minute and he was on the phone for hours. To call a halt to that, we had to buy him a mobile phone to use instead.

'Now,' she said and smiled sweetly. 'It was very naughty of you to steal the other boy's cigarettes, so Jim will buy you ten pounds' worth of tobacco every week!'

I was rather taken aback and said, 'That's illegal!'

'We have an addicted child here!' She stormed, lecturing me. 'You will have to buy him ten pounds' worth of tobacco every week!'

Our social worker nodded to me in agreement. Even though it went against the grain, (me being a non-smoker who has never smoked,) I had to do it!

As she was leaving, she handed him her card, and taking hold of him by his shoulders, smiled into his face; how wonderful he must have thought she was.

'Here is my number! Any time you need me, just call and if I'm not in the office, I'll get straight back to you!' She said and left.

He made numerous calls to her office; she never ever got back to him!

Social workers like her do untold damage to the system, building hostility in carers and distrust in the children. It made me ask myself, 'Is she actually worse than Ronald?' Then I thought, 'She is, isn't she?'

However, on the first occasion I took him along to the second, nearby restaurant, he chatted with the men serving while I placed an order for June and me.

I said, 'A small donor kebab and a small shish kebab please!' I turned to the boy and said, 'What would you like?'

The man serving said, 'He's already told me exactly what he wants,' and he did him a huge mixed kebab; I was rather gobsmacked at his rudeness.

However, they took quite a shine to him and said that he could call in tomorrow. The following day he caught a bus in time for them opening at around 11.00 am. That evening, he stayed with them until after 6.00 pm and the last bus had gone, so one of the men brought him to the house.

I said, 'He has got our number; I would have gone for him.'

The man dismissed it with a wave of his hand. 'It's okay, no problem. If you bring him on Sunday at ten o'clock, we'll take him with us, we go to the football every Sunday.'

When we went in, June said she would make supper for him.

He said, 'not hungry, had kebabs.'

During the months, up until he moved to his uncle's place, he made the bus journey every morning and was welcomed by them. They wouldn't take anything for his kebabs, or for bringing him home. They had my number, but, as if family, they brought him home many times at around 6.30 pm. As there was no transport on Sundays, I dropped him off every week to go to football. They wouldn't take any money off us for taking him either. They fed him several meals every single day and brought him home on Sundays too; I began to wonder if they were fostering him. Judging by the massively increased pile of dog-ends that he chucked around the garden, they had to be buying him tobacco as well, on top of the lot I was buying for him.

It was quite odd, how he finally did move to his uncle's place. He was just coming sixteen in a few months when he packed his case, walked out of the door and was gone. Of course, we reported it but we never heard anything further. A couple of months later we went to the restaurant again for our supper. The men were so pleased to see us and greeted us with a smile. The head man said, 'Hello, hello; any word from the boy?'

'No,' I said, 'Has he been in touch with you?'

His smile faded and shaking his head he said in a disappointed tone of voice. 'No, not a word.'

I thought that painted a very accurate picture of him; take all and give nothing!

The one good thing that came out of his move was: we never saw his awful social worker again; thank goodness! So, we carried on where we left off.

New breed.

We had another (boy?) from somewhere in Africa, and the most bizarre (seventeen?) year old I have ever encountered. I would say that he was the fore-runner in a new breed of particularly horrible type of (child?) He was assessed by the authorities as being a young teenager, but we very soon realised we were dealing with an adult, probably mid to late-twenties. Upon arrival, he was quite pleasant and became very interested in the photo of a group of Karate students with their teacher.

'Yes,' June said, 'That's my son Peter. He's the Karate teacher and we go to his club every Thursday evening; would you like to come along?'

He eagerly agreed, so we took him and Peter said he hadn't got a Karate suit to fit him, but he could have one for the following week. He stripped off, down to his tee shirt and joggers to take part. Peter was pleased with how he had done saying that he had done extremely well, so that was a good start. He seemed very happy and I said it would be much better next week, he would have the proper gear; he smiled and nodded.

When they arrive, nearly all of these (kids?) have a phone, sometimes even three phones, all with different sim cards which gives them choices of free access to friends or relations who have different sim cards. They are very well tutored in exactly what gets results, and if they have doubts, their phones are linked to someone who will very soon give them guidance and put them in the picture. Then invariably, they dictate what they are entitled to.

When we arrived home, he went to his bedroom and we could hear him talking on his phone in his own language. Straight away his behaviour changed completely. He refused to have a shower, and that was after what had been a quite strenuous workout. He refused to eat his supper, then got into bed fully clothed and refused to get up the next day. June finally managed to get him out of bed at dinner time, and again, he refused to eat or drink. We took him to a restaurant, along with our other boy and as it was Friday, I handed our boy his pocket money. The African young man was at the far end of the table, so I asked our boy if he would pass his pocket money along. The other one folded his arms, turned his back and refused it. Our boy was shocked and kept saying, 'But it's your money.' Still, he wouldn't take it.

I got up and approached him, 'What would you like to eat?'

He turned his back on me then went and stood in the middle of the restaurant with his arms folded and we proceeded with our meal. Later, I threw the untouched meal that I bought for him into the bin. His odd behaviour continued all day. As it was a really hot day, I suggested stopping at a country pub, thinking: 'We could have a shandy and the boys might appreciate a Coke.' Once again, he sat with his back to us, arms folded and staring into space. Again, he left the drink that I bought. That evening, he walked out of the front door and was gone. As is required when a child goes missing, we informed social services, and the police.

Hours later, the police phoned to say that they had picked him up many miles away and they were bringing him back to the house.

Very much later June said, 'The police are outside.'

I went to investigate and found him grappling with a policeman in the drive. Because the policeman was trying to get him to go into the house, they almost came to blows. The policeman was on his own and must have felt that he couldn't cope, so he called for backup. Shortly afterwards, two policewomen arrived and entered the house in a very official manner. The first one, a big lady, strutted in and with a sour expression, glanced at June, then scowling at me and as though disgusted, said brusquely, 'He's refusing to come in; has he been abused?'

Before I had a chance to reply, she looked at our other boy who was standing nearby and was quite distressed by the goings on. 'Are you fostered here?' She asked.

'Yes.' He replied softly.

We got the impression that she was here to rescue these unfortunate children from their wicked foster parents; and still scowling, she nodded towards the door, 'He says he doesn't want to be here, do you want to leave this place?' She asked, as though expecting him to say yes.

'No, I do not!' He replied, 'I'm very happy here; he needs to go!'

A couple of hours later, the policeman came in and said, 'I have spoken to him on the telephone, through 'Language Line,' and also to an Out-of-Hour's social worker. They have given him their assurances that, first thing in the morning, an alternative arrangement will be made and they will come for him!'

I nodded approval, 'Okay.'

He then said to June, 'Can he stay the night? He told Language Line that he hasn't had any food or drink for over a day. Do you think you could make him something to eat?'

June said, 'I have no objection to him staying, or feeding him. He has been offered food many times but has refused to eat or drink, in fact, I have just thrown the meal I made earlier for him in the bin, it was untouched.'

Thinking that speed was of the essence, she very quickly rustled up, fresh eggs, (from our very own chickens,) beans on toast and tea. By that time, it was around 1.00 am. The policeman brought him in and we all, police women included, gawked in amazement when he walked straight through the kitchen to his bedroom, once again refusing to eat or drink.

By the time we were going to bed, it was gone 2.00 am and June said, 'You know I've pre-booked to go to that championship dog show tomorrow, would it be okay if I left him with you? The social worker will be here first thing in the morning.'

'Hmm,' I said, 'No problem.'

The next morning, June was long gone, so at around 8.30 am, I knocked his door and placed his breakfast on the side in his room. Lying fully clothed on his bed, he gave me an angry glare but didn't speak. The hours ticked by and it was lunch time; still no Social Worker! I made lunch, took it to his room and removed his untouched breakfast.

At around 2.30 pm; still no sign of the social worker! I was having tea with my mother-in-law who was staying with us, and is quite forgetful as she suffers with Alzheimer's. We were rather shocked when he literally staggered through the kitchen and went out of the front door. I went after him and implored him to please come back and wait for the social worker, but he blustered on and went down the road. I returned and phoned social services. They kept me on the phone for quite a while taking details. Straight after the phone call, I searched the house for my Mother-in-law, she was nowhere to be found. By the time I'd searched the house and the garden, I was quite alarmed and distressed. I dashed out to see where the boy had gone. He was around a hundred metres down the road, lying prostrate, with his legs on the pavement and his body, from just below his buttocks, stretched out into the road, and his arms above his head, fully extended towards the centre of the road leaving about a metre between him and the white line. To my horror, my mother-in-law was standing in the middle of the road, by the white line, pleading with him, in an attempt to persuade him to come back to the house. Cars were skirting around them and whizzing by. He just laid there, fully aware that she could be in serious danger, but he was determined to carry his plan through, no matter what the cost to anyone else. I was so shocked and I have to say, absolutely disgusted.

I ushered her back to the safety of the house and returned to the (boy?) Several speeding cars stopped and reversed back to ask if he was okay. Even several neighbours came out and asked if he was okay.

I said, 'He is refusing to get up! I can't manhandle him up and back to the house, I would be in serious trouble if I did that!'

My friend arrived to service my van, and upon seeing him lying there said, 'Good God! How do you think a driver will feel if he hits him? This is a very dangerous road! I know it's only supposed to be forty along here, but they go hell for leather, don't they? By the way, my boy says your phone is ringing.'

I dashed back to the house, and updated social services as to what was going on and returned as quickly as possible.

Upon my return, my friend said, 'He says he wants a doctor.'

I turned to the boy and for the umpteenth time said, 'Will you please get up and come back to the house?'

'Dactar, Dactar,' he said.

'Please get up and come back to the house and I shall phone for a doctor!' I said.

With that he started to rise. My friend and I supporting him, practically carried him back to the house. While I was looking up the Doctor's number and about to call for a doctor, the phone rang again and it was social services.

'He says he wants a doctor.' I told them and I called for a doctor straight after.

An ambulance turned up with a Medic on his own. He went to his bedroom and after examining him, came back to the kitchen where my friends and I were.

'Huh!' He said, 'he's healthier than you and me.'

I showed him some drawings and writing that he had done with the aid of a small interpreting machine. He looked at it in amazement; the content was extremely bizarre, and when I saw it, it made me feel really uneasy about him actually being in our house, especially after his behaviour today.

The Medic said, 'I can't take him in for a check up on my own, you'll have to come with me!'

I shook my head. 'I'm sorry I can't do that! My mother-in-law has Alzheimer's and can't be left alone.'

My friend, because of the goings on, had foregone the servicing of my van, and with his son had joined me in the kitchen for a cup of tea. The medic pointed at them: 'Can one of them come?'

My friend said, 'we're only visitors here, we can't go!'

The Medic then phoned the hospital and they were quite rattled that there was no one to accompany him. Finally, they reluctantly agreed that the Medic could take him on his own. I didn't assist in getting him to the ambulance as at that vital moment, social services rang again. After updating them, they said they wanted to speak to the Medic. I glanced at my friend, 'Where's the medic?'

He nodded towards the door, 'He's taken him!'

I told them he had gone and they hung up. Ten minutes later, they phoned back. 'We've been in touch with the hospital and they've no record of any one of his description there.'

'They won't even be there yet,' I said, 'The hospital is three quarters of an hour from us.'

June arrived home and I told her what had happened. She was aghast but then said, 'Well, anyway, at least he's gone.'

Much later, the hospital rang again. 'Can you come and collect him?'

I said, 'I can't do that, we can't have him back here, we're not able to keep him safe!'

The lady doctor was quite indignant. 'Why? What has he done?'

I explained the situation and gave her a full description of his behaviour earlier, but still she seemed quite irate. Later on, she phoned again and June took the call. June told her that he was social services responsibility, they needed to decide where they would take him. He couldn't come back here as we weren't able to keep him safe. The lady doctor was really annoyed and reported us to social services for refusing to take a young boy back. The impression we got from her attitude was: she seemed to think that he was a very nice young man; exactly what we thought, initially.

Social services did an investigation for a period of **six months**. Finally, it went to Panel and they decided that we had acted appropriately, so we were reinstated, but boy did that get up my nose! What about the Social worker who assured him, us and the police, that an alternative placement would be arranged and he would be collected first thing in the morning, then failed to materialise? Was she investigated for six months? I don't think so! It made me feel really resentful and when speaking to other carers who have been doing this for years, invariably they say that they are frustrated and distressed how things are handled, in a lot of cases by social workers who 'Haven't got a clue!'

Speaking of people who haven't got a clue; we had another boy, supposedly sixteen but we very soon surmised that he had to be mid to late-twenties. This one also hailed from Africa. When these so-called kids arrive, they usually have the clothes that they stand up in, so a clothing allowance is allocated that we would normally use to buy items of their choosing, such as: tee shirts, trousers or joggers, pyjamas, socks, under clothes and trainers etc. However, along with him, came his allocated social worker and with her numerous directives she brusquely said, 'Oh, that's not the way it's done! Give him the money! Let him buy his own clothes!'

We were very sceptical about this arrangement, but we complied. The result? A ninety-five-pound pair of trainers! Brilliant! That of course meant that there were insufficient funds left to buy necessary basic items.

As you can probably gather, we have fostered children regarded as among the most highly disturbed children in the UK. This young man fell into the category of what we began to term as the 'new breed.' June said that in all her years of fostering, he was one of the most stressful placements that we've ever had. It seemed to me that his social worker was the catalyst orchestrating his horrible behaviour. He knew that if it was bad enough, he would in the end, be sent to where **he** wanted to be... London; where else?

A lot of boys and girls that we had previously, had an excellent social worker who took on the task in a very firm way, and didn't tolerate the rubbish that this one apparently condoned and even encouraged. Owing to his totally obnoxious behaviour, he was going to be moved to another place; 'could we drop him off at ten forty-five?'

At that time, we had other boys, so they had to come along as well. We left straight after breakfast to make the two-hour journey. I thought it would be a good idea to stop at the motorway services so that we could all have a drink. As it was quite early; before 10.00 am. Everyone said a Coke was fine. We arrived at the drop off ten minutes early; 10.35 am. We knew there were other young people at this new place and assumed, as he would no longer be our responsibility, he would be having lunch with them. Upon our arrival, the man in charge who answered the door, was perplexed. 'Who was I and what did I want? And this young man with the bag; what is he doing here?'

I did my utmost to put him in the picture. The (boy's) social worker hadn't even been in touch with them to inform them that the young man was coming! I had to wait alone, in silence, in a room with the young man for over half an hour, while the man in charge made a number of phone calls in order to establish exactly what was going on, and because of his previous behaviour, again, I felt extremely uncomfortable.

By the time we left him with them, it was just after 11.15am. Later on, his highly indignant, (very efficient?) social worker phoned ours and dictated exactly what he was entitled to: 'They left him without any food and they didn't bring his bedding!' She said.

Our social worker said, 'bedding? That's a new one on me, I've never heard of that!'

Our lunch time was almost two hours away, usually around 1.00 pm and in all our years of fostering, no one has **ever** arrived with bedding!

Upon our return, we discovered that he had destroyed several quite valuable items including a particularly nice chair that he had scribbled all over with a biro. I felt that getting him off our hands was cheap at the price because, next step, an allegation?

Unfortunately, there is no redress with these so-called kids and they know it! They are fully aware that they have the power, they have been well tutored on exactly what gets results and if you are damaged in the process; tough!

Another (boy?) that we had during the debacle with the African boy, also assessed to be age fifteen and we reckoned he was also at least mid-twenties.

I appreciate that it is very difficult for someone in their mid-twenties to masquerade as a fifteen-year-old. However, I assumed that he took his cue from the African young man, and in turn started behaving in a totally obnoxious manner. What sparked it all off was: I told him that the last bus home from the town, was very early, so I usually made the journey (14 miles round trip) every evening at 6.30pm to collect the others, including some other foster carers' children, who usually went in for language classes, and I dropped them off on the way home. Would he please be there? I waited over half an hour with the other young people in the car and he never turned up. At around 9.00pm he rang the house and didn't ask, but told me to come and pick him up. I stressed that when I collect the others, he should make it his business to be there. I think I was talking to myself, as each night we had a repeat performance.

I wasn't feeling very well and anyway, I'd had quite enough of this, so on the fifth night, when he phoned, I said, 'Get a taxi home! We shall pay the fare at the door and dock it from your pocket money.'

That enraged him and he arrived home in a seething temper. I met the taxi at the door and while I paid the fare, he dashed into the house. I followed shortly afterwards and he was in the living room. I approached and stood behind June's chair. Our other foster boy was sitting nearby while she, trying to reason with him regarding his behaviour, said: 'Do you realise that people are dying while attempting to get what you have here? You have a perfectly good, warm home, a clean bed, good food and -'

He flew into a rage and screamed: '- No English, Mother fucker!'

He stormed out of the room, shouted 'Mother fucker' again, kicked his bedroom door open and slammed it shut with all his might. I was quite gobsmacked until June said, 'This isn't the first time he has done this; he did the same thing a couple of days ago.'

She pointed at our other boy, 'he was here that time as well. Do you think he would have hit me if you weren't here?'

I shudder to think what would have happened if he had hit her!

Generally, people in this country don't use the expression 'Mother fucker.' He certainly didn't get it from us; it's very American, used regularly in movies and it actually disgusts me. What I found really odd was; he used it while he was addressing a woman? Our other boy, a really nice young man agreed with our age assessment of him, and he said he was disgusted as well.

A week or so later, we had a review for the (boy?) during which, he said that I had called him a 'Mother fucker' and he also told his friends that I had done so. His friends asked our boy why I had called him it and our boy told us that he said: 'Jim did not say that; I was there and I heard everything; he shouted it at Mummy.'

Once again, we had an allegation. I was fortunate that our other boy had been present, although it didn't exonerate me, all it did was cast doubt on his (and our) story. When the social workers left, June said, 'I don't think they believed him when he said that you called him a 'mother fucker,' do you?'

I glanced at the ceiling and thought: 'The old adage comes to mind; there's no smoke without fire!'

Everyone, when talking to their children, raises their voice, uses their hands to express points and challenges bad behaviour, but you can't treat these (kids?) as you would your own. You mustn't raise your voice; that can be classed as shouting. Don't wave your hands! That can be seen as threatening behaviour, and you must not challenge them. So, what do you do? Grin and bear it and let them carry on regardless?

Some time ago, we attended a meeting and a very high-ranking social worker was talking to us privately regarding a difficult placement and said, 'You have to look after your business! Yours is the only business where you are guilty until proven innocent! You have to be very careful with these children! If they, or even someone else makes an allegation against you, it can ruin your business! Why, I know of a carer who was struck off for six weeks because of an allegation that turned out to be false!'

'Huh!' June said, 'We were under investigation for six months!'

The Social worker was right, this is in effect a business, and that business is dependent on the luck of the draw. If you are fortunate enough to get a 'good' social worker, it can be wonderful! However, when you are placed a child, and with that child, along comes someone like Ronald, it can be soul destroying!

Carol and Jackie, our fostering friends were discussing this 'business,' and Carol said that they had given over forty years of their lives to fostering, and of course we had done the same. We were all in agreement that it has been rewarding; although, if, on occasions, you are stuck with a Social Worker interested in ticking boxes, covering their own backside and making sure you know who is boss, it can be excruciatingly painful and utterly frustrating. It is unlike any other job in more ways than one. It's not nine to five, rather a twenty-four-seven job, as you have to be available day and night. Carol said that after a lifetime devoted to most professions, at the end there is normally some sort of recognition, reward, or security, but fostering? Even though you have done specialist training, accrued skills that are unique and give you an insight into life in general, and empathy for the child in care, you are not a Social Worker, you are not actually employed by the Authority. There is no golden handshake, no pension, in fact, there is absolutely nothing other than perhaps a bunch of flowers! I can't think of any other profession where this happens; can you? If you are sick, or you stop fostering, due for example to an allegation, that's exactly what you get; nothing!

It used to be that when the child or children that you have fostered reach eighteen, their 'caring' authority let them go. There invariably was no further support as they were now 'out of care,' and that was the very reason a number of them ended up having problems or even in prison! All of the nurturing is gone and they have to manage on a shoe string. No matter what sort of support they provide, in a lot of cases, being in care, especially residential care, leaves that indelible mark. We strived to nurture the children through these difficult times and we still support, in more ways than financial, kids that we took on all those years ago, because we couldn't, just let them go! We did and still do actually 'care' for them. Unfortunately, that was a flaw in our makeup and on occasions, made us vulnerable to emotional blackmail.

However, on the occasions that we see, or are in touch with ex foster children, just as with our own children, it is such a pleasure. So, in that sense, there are no regrets. Many of them enriched our lives beyond what we could ever have dreamt, and when I think back, it brings a smile, but the same can't be said for some of the social workers, although I have to say, there were some who we found working with an absolute pleasure, and we still regard them as dear friends. Sadly, they were the exception rather than the rule.

Epilogue.

All in all, what do I think about fostering? Well, how I see all of this is: when you reach the end as we have, it leaves something of an emptiness that makes me wonder exactly what have we been doing all these years? The other thing to consider is: looking back on all of what we went through, the skills that we developed, and the preparation for life it gave our children from a very early age; do I find it odd that not one of them took up fostering? No, I do not!

So, there you have it, if you think you want to foster, best be prepared for the good times, and the bad.

Jim Bryans.

www.ingramcontent.com/pod-product-compliance
Lightning Source LLC
LaVergne TN
LVHW051216070526
838200LV00063B/4924